HEY, HEY WE'RE

THE MONKEES

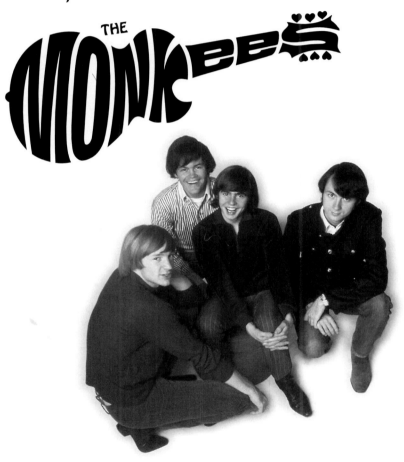

EDITED BY

Harold Bronson

CAST OF CHARACTERS:

Micky Dolenz. . . . . Monkee
Davy Jones . . . . Monkee
Peter Tork. . . . . Monkee
Michael Nesmith . . . . Monkee
Bob Rafelson . . . . Producer/Director
Ward Sylvester. . . . . Producer/Manager
Tommy Boyce. . . . . Producer/Songwriter
Bobby Hart. . . . . Producer/Songwriter
Don Kirshner . . . . Music Supervisor
Jeff Barry. . . . . Producer
Chip Douglas . . . . Producer
James Frawley . . . . Director
Henry Diltz . . . . Photographer
Hank Cicalo . . . . Recording Engineer
Stephen Stills . . . . Musician
Peter Noone . . . . Singer
Bill Chadwick. . . . . Songwriter/Tour Manager

Publisher: W. Quay Hays
Editor: Harold Bronson
Design: Phillis Stacy
Editorial Assistant: Sarah Diamond

For Information:
General Publishing Group, Inc.
2701 Ocean Park Boulevard, Suite 140
Santa Monica, California 90405

Library of Congress Catalog Card Number 96-077591

Printed in the USA
10 9 8 7 6 5 4 3 2 1

General Publishing Group
Los Angeles

INTRODUCTION

In Micky Dolenz's less profound moments he tosses off *The Monkees* as a mere TV show about a rock band, equating his role as a drummer to that of Spock on another well-known TV series. "Leonard Nimoy wasn't really a Vulcan, but he played one on *Star Trek*."

Putting the impact of the music in perspective, he recounts a story of a fan who approached him after a Monkees concert. The young girl was bewildered by the seriousness of Micky's new protest song "Mommy and Daddy," which dealt with the plight of the Indian: "She had tears in her eyes as she walked up to me and asked why we didn't record any of the good old songs you can dance to. I realized what had happened and what the Monkees were all about. They were what a first-grade teacher is to a child learning math. You can't teach a kid to multiply until you teach him to add. The reason the Monkees were so successful was because we filled a gap. The Beatles and all the other groups were trying to appeal to a sophisticated audience. Nobody was playing to the kids. We gave them something to listen to."

In Micky's more profound moments, he realizes that the Monkees had a larger social significance because they brought long hair into the living room. "Up until then, anyone with long hair was thought to be a doper or hippie hoodlum. Even though the Beatles wore long hair, their comments about acid and politics gave it a negative connotation. The kids said, 'See the Monkees, they just wanna laugh and have fun and play.' It then became difficult for the parents to deny them: 'Well, alright, if the Monkees do it, it's okay.'"

TV show, rock band, cultural phenomenon, the Monkees were all of these, but much more, and therein lies the confusion of how they are considered. First off, *The Monkees* was a TV show. Although they were acting in fictitious stories, Micky Dolenz, Davy Jones, Michael Nesmith and Peter Tork were essentially playing themselves and using their own names in the series. They were chosen, in part, because they had musical ability. Hired to play a rock band, they actually became a rock band. They toured and even recorded a couple of albums, performing as a self-contained unit.

Their first two quintuple-million-selling albums proved controversial, featuring only the Monkees' voices and not their instrumental performances. Originally, the producers hadn't expected them to play, and now that they wanted to, the project's music supervisor, Don Kirshner, didn't feel the need to revise his successful formula. Nesmith and Tork, who considered themselves musicians primarily, were frustrated and alienated by the recording process. However, they were naively unaware that many top rock bands of the day— Paul Revere & the Raiders, Herman's Hermits and the Beach Boys, among them—invariably used studio musicians to record their instrumental backing tracks. As head Hermit Peter Noone said, "For us it was primarily a financial decision. We made most of our money on the road. So it cost us money to be in the studio learning and recording the songs, and we were contractually committed to supplying MGM with 48 masters a year. We were fortunate to have the talents of Jimmy Page, John Paul Jones and the other studio musicians to record our backing tracks."

Of equal importance to the music was the TV show. Producer/director Bob Rafelson, influenced by France's New Wave in cinema, bettered his Beatles model in creating a TV series that runs circles around most of what airs today. Its quality and innovation didn't go unnoticed at the time, and the show garnered two Emmy awards in its first season.

The Monkees' feature-length movie *Head* took too many chances in tone, structure and an experimental marketing campaign to result in anything but a bomb. Ahead of its time for many years, it's now considered a classic. Whole gaggles of the curious—from the Rolling Stones to George Lucas' film students—descended upon Schneider and Rafelson's screening room to view the film.

It's the high quality of the records that is the primary reason for the continuing interest in the Monkees. At press time, recent covers of Monkees' songs, "A Little Bit Me, A Little Bit You" and "Steppin' Stone" have been released by the Specials and P.J. & Duncan, respectively, and the Sex Pistols are performing "Steppin' Stone" on their reunion tour. The Monkees benefited from Don Kirshner's stable of the top writers of the day, including Gerry Goffin & Carole King, Neil Diamond, Harry Nilsson and Tommy Boyce & Bobby Hart. The production was perfect, and at times inspired. And the Monkees successfully conveyed their personalities in their vocals, an asset not lost on producer Jeff Barry: "When I produced Micky singing 'I'm a Believer,' I was struck by how differently he sang from anybody I had worked with before. With most singers the words are vehicles for the notes. But Micky, being an actor, added an extra, dramatic quality.

As writers, the Monkees proved to be no slouches either. Although Nesmith missed the Top 10 with the group, the songs he composed around this time scored a handful of hits for himself, Linda Ronstadt, the Nitty Gritty Dirt Band and, in 1988, a cover of "Mary, Mary" for rap group Run-D.M.C. The underachiever Dolenz scored the Monkees' second biggest hit in Britain with "Randy Scouse Git," a non-U.S.-released single. The unconfident Tork composed a song that the TV producers selected to accompany the end credits during the second season.

Complementing the cutting-edge innovation of the TV show, the members stretched the boundaries of their recordings. Nesmith, arguably, invented country rock when he introduced the feel to "Papa Gene's Blues" on the first album. Dolenz acquired one of the first Moog synthesizers in the country and in June, 1967, played it on the Monkees recording of "Daily Nightly." When Jack Nicholson compiled the soundtrack album for *Head*, he broke new ground by interspersing dialogue between the songs.

Oddly enough, despite the quandary of considering them a legitimate rock band, apropos of Micky's earlier observation many performers with stacks of hit records, among them Tom Petty, Pat Benatar and R.E.M.'s Michael Stipe, cite the Monkees as a larger influence than the Beatles. And their impact on popular culture continues to be referenced: Jim Carrey's character in *Dumb & Dumber* remembers the Monkees as having influenced the Beatles; in a flashback on *The Simpsons*, Marge is traumatized when a fellow student criticizes the group after eyeing her Monkees lunch box; Davy Jones' presence infuses both *Brady Bunch* movies; and in Japan, the original recording of "Daydream Believer," a song that originally appealed to young teens, accompanies a TV beer advertisement.

In order to commemorate the Monkees' 30th Anniversary, I wanted to compile a photo history. To accompany the photos, I thought it would be more appropriate to let the Monkees themselves express how they felt about their experiences. Their thoughts are complemented by those who aided their efforts in the recording studio as well as on the TV set. Most of the interviews were edited from ones conducted for the Monkees documentary airing on the Disney channel and for a CD-ROM.

With a tour and a new album that finds the four reunited in the studio for the first time since the 1960s, the history is far from over.

—Harold Bronson

Bob Rafelson and Bert Schneider

THE
BEGINNING

I had the idea for the Monkees years before the Beatles arrived. I wrote it as a pilot for Universal in 1960. It was about a folk-group—something about which I knew, because I was traveling with a group of four unruly and chaotic musicians in Mexico in 1953. I used many of the incidents that happened to me in Mexico when I was seventeen years old in *The Monkees* episodes.

-Bob Rafelson

Bert Schneider had been the treasurer of Screen Gems. His father was the president of Columbia Pictures. In that capacity, he had purchased Nevins-Kirshner Music, so there was now a pop music division, and a commercial company called Elliot Under An Elliot. Bert was trying to find a show that would take advantage of some of the new strengths that had just come to the company. It was not lost on us that *A Hard Day's Night* had been directed by Richard Lester who had come from the background of commercials. The thought was that a show incorporating pop music and this radical new style of filmmaking would be innovative, and that's how they came to the idea of what became the television version of the Beatles. That was, really, Rafelson's original idea for it. Once having made that choice, they started thinking, "Should we use a pre-existing group?" Herman's Hermits was big at the time. But, if you used an existing group, you were subject to their previous recording and other contracts. We wouldn't have control.

In those days, groups were self-selecting. And they didn't select people very different from themselves.

Network television was even more of a mass medium than it is now. There were only three networks, and only the largest cities had an independent station or two. To succeed on network television, you had to attract at least thirty percent of the audience. The thought was that our group had to be demographically diverse. You can't have four guys who are all the same. By that time they had brought in the writers of the pilot, Paul Mazursky and Larry Tucker. The four prototypes they came up with were a country and western singer with a Will Rogers/Herb Shriner kind of feel; certainly a young English boy because of the British Invasion and because I already managed David; a clown, a Jerry Lewis prototype; and a shy, awkward teenager—Huntz Hall from the Bowery Boys was the prototype for that. We thought that most adolescent girls need only bond with one person in a group. You don't enhance the group much by having three or four guys they can particularly bond to—they're gonna choose one anyway. So if we have four very different guys, we will have a much broader demographic base. The way to judge how well we did our job, of course, is that you hope that twenty-five percent of the audience

would choose each of the guys. I think, because there had been so much attention given to the open auditions, that people thought that we looked at a whole bunch of people indiscriminately, and we chose the four that we thought were the most talented or had the nicest smiles. It really was more considered than that.

-Ward Sylvester

To get things rolling, Ward and I would go around to different clubs looking for prospective members for the TV show. We saw Sonny and Cher and The Byrds on one bill, and across the street was little Stevie Wonder. We went to see Arthur Lee and Love—this is all in one night. The guitar player from Love, a tall, good-looking blond guy, we thought would be good for the show. The Monkees vests and yellow shirts that we wore in our pilot came from what Sonny Bono was wearing. We saw the MFQ—the Modern Folk Quartet—with Chip Douglas; we looked at Jerry Yester as a potential candidate. Word was getting around, and people like Paul Peterson and Paul Williams, and actors from across the country were buzzing about this. They decided to have open auditions, so they put the Madness ad in Variety: *Madness!! Musicians, singers for acting roles in a new TV series—spirited Ben Frank's-types.* Ben Frank's was a restaurant on Sunset, a late night place to get your eggs and bacon after you've been out on the razzle. And so Ben Frank types were long-haired, sort of beatnik weirdos from the sixties. During the day it was a normal, eggs-over-easy place. But at night, it was a hangout, like Canters down on Fairfax Avenue. Bert wanted strange types; he wanted raw, new stuff that he alone could bring in. He's a strange old bird.

-*Davy Jones*

We saw Mike first, hosting New Talent Night at The Troubadour, a folk rock club that still exists. The job required a great deal of grace because the quality of the acts was very uneven. They more or less let anybody who wanted to come up and perform. He did it with a marvelous amount of poise and wit and was able to walk that very narrow line between allowing the audience to understand the humor of it without really putting down the performers. Michael has always had a lot of class, and a maturity, even at that age, in his very early twenties. He also had a wife and child, so he grew up faster. I first saw Micky performing in a bowling alley with a group called the Missing Links. Micky did seem to me to be the Jerry Lewis-like clown we were looking for. He was always on. He was very inventive and clever with a wonderful mind twist. And he was the only one who had episodic television experience, with *Circus Boy*, which we thought would be a plus. Peter was the most interesting one in the sense that the character he played was the least like himself. I think that the other guys played characters very close to who they really were. Peter's character had a gentle innocence and a little slow-wittedness about him. Peter has the gentle innocence, but he is not at all slow-witted. It's interesting, even though Huntz Hall was the prototype for Peter, what most reminds me of his character is Norman Drabble of the Kevin Fagen comic strip. It's called *Drabble* and is about a college student who is well meaning but a little fumbling. He's always embarrassed and always says the wrong thing. And Peter was able to play that. Peter is very intelligent and very well-educated. He always surprises me with allusions to classical music and to classical literature. He's very spiritual and very insightful. He had to suppress an awful lot of that to be the Peter that we know from television.

-Ward Sylvester

To my way of thinking, the thing that sets *The Monkees* apart from all the other TV shows about the youth culture of its time was that Bert was a fan. He was a fan of the Beatles. He liked the spirit of the times. It wasn't just another fad for an out-of-touch producer to cash in on. That's the impression I got from everybody else who made TV shows. He took the big chance. In the pilot, you'll remember, "We'll take the boys down to the club—an old Army buddy of mine is manager of the record store—the manager of the group...." And he was going to be a continuing character, and they dumped him. They opted for no adult authority figure in the show at all. And that, as far as I know, hadn't been done before, and not again until the 1980s, when the British show *The Young Ones* played on MTV. Up until then, shows like *Father Knows Best* and *My Three Sons* always had adults. That was one thing that never could have happened if Bert had been a cigar-chomping, older executive: "I don't understand this, but the kids'll love it...."

-Peter Tork

I interviewed for three or four shows that month, because it was pilot season. There were other shows about music that they were trying to get on the air, one about a Beach Boys kind of act, and another like Peter, Paul and Mary. But this one was by far the most unique. And I remember thinking, "I really want this one. This is kind of cool."

The whole thing was different. Whereas most shows at the time were being produced by middle-aged executives, Bert Schneider and Bob Rafelson were only around thirty years old. They were part of the pop culture, and they had a different attitude. My first interview was very unusual. I walked into this office and there were pizza cartons and coke cans everywhere, and these two guys were sitting around in jeans and t-shirts and I thought they were gofers; I thought they were the guys who brought in the pizza. But they were the producers. So that was a big difference for someone like myself who had been to a lot of auditions in Hollywood; it was usually an older guy in a suit with a cigar. Bert and Bob were much looser. Although I don't remember this, I've been told that I picked up on the vibe and went over and took one of the many empty coffee cups that were all over the place and moved it over and went "Check." They laughed, and the rest is a hysterectomy.

-Micky Dolenz

When I auditioned for *The Monkees*, I sang and hung out for a while. They called me the next day to tell me that they were interested and could I come another day. When I came in, I got the feeling that they thought I was gonna happen, and they wanted to keep contact somehow, being up and coming Hollywood moguls. They were polite, and I sensed that they were more interested in me as a person. I was real up front with them. I said, "Basically, I'm not that interested in the show, but mainly I want to write the songs because that's where the moola is." And then I said, "Listen, I know another guy that's a lot like me and he's probably a little brighter, and he might be a little bit quicker and funnier." I had had that beaten into me by this guy in New York, for reasons that still escape me, that I was not funny, and I should not try to be funny. That's when I suggested Peter Tork.

-Stephen Stills

I was playing piano at the Golden Bear for Steve Stills and Ron Long, who were called The Buffalo Fish. Steve was my buddy from Greenwich Village; we knew each other because we were the kids who looked alike. When I was on the way out, Steve called me over and said, "Peter, I've just met this guy who is doing a TV show based on *A Hard Day's Night*. You should try out." I dismissed the idea, "Yeah, yeah." He said, "Peter, this is Steve. You really should go try out for this thing." "Oh, all right." So I got on the bus in Huntington Beach and schlepped all the way to Hollywood for the auditions. Up until then, I hadn't done anything except for a couple of hootenannies at the Troubadour, where, incidentally, I met Mike. I thought that because I knew Steve Sills, and he knew Bob Rafelson, that I was going to get special entree into the auditioning process. I walked in—"Take a seat, please." I waited like everybody else. Mike came in and said, "Hello, Pete." One kid did get special treatment. Davy Jones walked through, like he owned the place. But I've grown to love him now. I do.

-Peter Tork

I played a simpleton. It was a character I had developed on the Greenwich Village stages as a way of protecting myself against the results of my bad jokes. "Of course you wouldn't like that joke because what kind of a fool I am." It just expanded from there.

-Peter Tork

Before we began filming, we went to the desert to shoot some commercials. They intelligently sent us out to do commercials first to get more of an idea how we'd interact, so they'd be better prepared for the television show. We had just met; we didn't know each other. Mike drove. He had recently bought a brand new Riviera Buick, which was then the hot car. During the trip, we didn't say much to each other. It was like, "Nice day." That was it. "Hungry?" "Yeah."

So we drove into this little restaurant, not speaking a word. We sat down, two by two in a booth, and ordered. Micky's and my salad came first. Just stick a fork in the bowl and whatever comes up goes in the mouth. Davy Jones says, "You pigs! Anyone would think you were raised in a barn, the way you guys are eatin'." Davy's salad finally came. He looked up at the waitress and said, "Thank you."

He didn't lift his eyes. I watched him. He took a knife and fork and cut the salad into one-inch strips, and cut the strips into one-inch squares, and poured the dressing on and tossed it until each and every one-inch square of lettuce was thoroughly soaked with blue cheese dressing. He politely put down his knife and fork. He then grabbed a handful of salad and smashed it in his face. Well, I broke up. We laughed and laughed. He looked up finally, with blue cheese dressing and squares of lettuce hanging off his face. He looked up at us. I think he was abashed—I mean we were abashed. He was flexing his muscles trying to see who we were and we just completely collapsed. He thought, "Maybe I've come on a little strong here. I need to make it right." He's an expert at that, boy. He's a very funny man.

-Peter Tork

There's nothing like smashing a couple of eggs over a friend's head and then some flour and a bit of rice pudding, you know. Food fights are great in the right place. Every time Micky has a meal, he has a food fight.

-Davy Jones

Michael was very kind to me at the outset. He put me up through the entire shooting of the pilot process. He and his wife had a wonderful little apartment just big enough for a guest on the day bed, which overlooked Hollywood. I remember a Thanksgiving Day when the air was crystal clear in a way that I've never seen it before or since in L.A., and you could see all the way out to Catalina. It was wonderful. That crystal clarity symbolizes the whole era for me. Mike and I wrote a few things together. We were very comradely and very buddy buddy, and it was a wonderful time, with Mike's then wife, Phyllis, and Christian, their little infant baby. The early days of the pilot shooting were just great by my lights and I had a wonderful time.

-Peter Tork

ike Elliot, who had done commercials in New York, directed the pilot. It was done in a quick-cut, in your face, Richard Lester style. People forget how conventional and slow-paced television was in the fifties and the early sixties. We wanted a commercial director because they were people who could tell a story or communicate a brief message in a minute. I bought for Screen Gems an audience research company called Audience Studies. They hooked up a psychogalvanometer to the audience's fingertips which purported to register how they were enjoying what they were seeing. In addition, they would have the audience twist dials from "we really like what we're seeing" to "we really don't like what we're seeing." A producer could presumably tell what scenes were working and what scenes weren't working. The networks were buying this as a kind of a pseudo-science. We took the pilot to Audience Studies and it was graded very poorly. We did focus groups afterward and people thought these were a bunch of smart-ass kids who had no respect for anybody. It was a disaster, the lowest-rated pilot they had ever tested. Rafelson's listening to the focus groups. They're getting the guys mixed up; they're saying Micky when they mean Davy. In the pilot, the Monkees are saving a girl's birthday party, which is a selfless mission. But in between, they're making fun of everybody and mouthing off. Rafelson said, "The problem is they don't know who these guys are. The pilot just opens and they're in the middle of this adventure and it's mad cap Marx Brothers characters but there's no feeling for who they are. I learned who they were from their screen tests. Let me

go back and run those screen tests first, so the audience meets the characters, one at a time, and knows who they are and sees that they are real people and charming and funny and nice." He recut the pilot and the ratings went through the roof. So we began using cinema verite and real interviews with the boys in the series. It was a great insight.

-Ward Sylvester

To me, they were just other actors; other people that were in the same show. I never really got to know them, even to this day. I've gotten to know Micky a little more over the last couple of years, but he was very aloof, very difficult to get close to. Peter was in another world: water beds, brown rice, Hare Krishna. He was scary. I didn't want to go to his house. I thought I'd be into some sort of orgy or some kind of drug den. I was kind of naive to all that stuff. Even Tommy Boyce and Bobby Hart, the songwriters, scared the pants off me.

-Davy Jones

The show very nearly didn't get on television because it was so out there. Long hair at that time was still synonymous with crimes against nature. *The Monkees* represented the pop culture, which was still considered an alternative lifestyle, a subculture. Some felt rock music was anti-American. I remember hearing stories that NBC was very concerned about showing long hair on kids on television. Network standards and practices said you had to have parental guidance. So, I think under duress, Bob and Bert put a manager in the pilot who ran a record store. When the pilot tested badly, Bob re-edited it and put in the interviews and took out the manager.

-Micky Dolenz

It was a hybrid show. We had, for instance, a camera man who was a complete hack. He knew how to do it the old way and he could do it in his sleep. The producers said they got him because they knew he could do lighting set-ups very quickly. He wouldn't do modern or original lighting, or anything special. He set each of the shots, although we had four and five times as many set-ups per day as normal. On *I Dream of Jeannie*, they cut every five or six seconds; sometimes we cut five or six times a second. So it required many more camera set-ups and we needed somebody who could crank that stuff out. The writers wrote conventional comedies, and they turned us loose on them. If it had been new from top to bottom— if the lighting had been new and the scripts had been avant garde—I don't think the show would have flown. Personally, I wish we would have done a third season because I think we were just coming into our own. We could have gotten more avant garde later on. I think our ability to cut up was finally getting to the producers, and they wanted to wash their hands of us.

-Peter Tork

It was too intense. The days were filled with being a Monkee. From 6:00 in the morning when my alarm went off to the time I got in my car down Sunset Boulevard at 6:30, quarter to 7:00, get on the set 7:15, start to get made up and the show was being filmed at 8:00, if we weren't laughing. We started laughing sometimes and we'd be laughing until 10:00 and they'd have to close the set down and we'd have to come back at 12:00. We had so much fun. We had sound men helping with electrical cables. We had the prop man in the scenes doing a prop. It was a different Hollywood. There were certain union rules, and it's important to have rules and certain procedures, but it was the free form that spilled off the stage into the people surrounding us. We had a lovely family of people working with us. And that's why we kept the free form that we had for the first year.

-Davy Jones

e were encouraged to be spontaneous and irreverent and not to treat this like the filming of a normal show. They didn't want four actors to merely come in and read their lines. They wanted to capture the irreverent and creative atmosphere that was happening at the time. To do that, you'd have to have an environment that in itself was quite structured, then let the wild animals loose in the middle, and that's what they did. It was crazy working under those circumstances. We used to drive people crazy, go through directors and kill assistant directors. They would die. Just cart them off and get a new one; it was brutal.

-Micky Dolenz

Micky had no real sense of humor when we first got together. He developed it. All of his jokes came from *The Reader's Digest*. I don't normally read *The Reader's Digest*—I normally read things in their entirety, complete with their complexity—but it just so happened that that was the magazine in my piano teacher's waiting room. So I knew all his jokes. Suddenly he turned around and decided he knew how to be funny, and he's now one of the funnier men around. I was talking to Jones shortly after we had been filming for a couple of months, and I said to him, "You know, Michael is really amazing. He really knows how to construct a joke. If the punch line isn't strong enough, he knows how to bring down the set-up so that it matches." The real key to humor is that the joke and the set-up match. And Michael knew how to master that. And Davy said, "Yeah, but he's not the funniest one of us." "Who is?" "Me." Micky was the funniest of us. Davy has since gotten funnier. I just stand in awe at those two comic geniuses.

-Peter Tork

Mike struck me as an incredibly witty, very funny purist. He was very spontaneous and had the ability to think on his feet, and I admired that. I was jealous of it. I found improvising difficult. Jim Frawley, from Second City, who was the primary director, trained us in improvisation for a few weeks before we started filming. I got a little more comfortable with it, but it was always tough for me, especially those interviews at the end of the show. As a trained actor, I was used to a script. I could improvise on the script, I could goof on it and have fun, but it was tough unless I had that script. Mike was always very good at that, so I learned a lot from him.

-Micky Dolenz

When we started filming, there were these three six-footers and then there was little me. Every time they went to do a floor shot, it was like, "Where is he?" So they used to say, "A man maker for Davy!" I hated that. And they'd bring a box and I'd stand on it.

-Davy Jones

We were on location at a farm, ready to shoot "Don't Look a Gift Horse in the Mouth." It was a half-hour away from shoot time, and the location guy from Screen Gems, a typical bureaucrat, said, "I went to the farm but there's no farmer." I said, "You paid him $500 for the use of the place. Go find him. He said, "I don't know what to do." I said, "Well, just jump over the fence and go knock on his door." He jumped over the fence and was told that the farmer was on the "back forty." He said, "I'm going down to the back forty." "Just knock the gate down," I said. "Oh! Screen Gems can't possibly allow anything like that!" I told him, "You go look for the farmer." He went and I took the first truck and rammed the gate, broke it open, and we marched in. After all, to pay for a gate was going to cost $500 and it was $10,000 an hour to shoot. In any event, I shot 125 set-ups the first day, breaking every record in television. That set a pattern of "Let these guys do what they do. They're mad, they're wild, but they have a definite way of going about things, and they know what they're doing."

-Bob Rafelson

BOYCE & HART

W̲e had worked on the pilot show for a year, and had been led to believe that we were going to produce the records. Once the show was sold, once there was NBC and RCA Records and Kelloggs and Yardley, Don Kirshner, who hadn't been involved for that first year of preparation, flew out and got involved, and that's when he broke the news to us one morning. "Although you guys have written a lot of hits, you have never really produced any. We need to go with producers who have proven track records. You're off the project as producers." We were devastated. We would hear the news from week to week of producers that they had tried. I believe Mickie Most and Phil Spector turned them down. Snuffy Garrett had a shot, and when they got the theme song back, somebody said it sounded like a Gary Lewis track, which wasn't surprising as he was having hits with him at the time. Then they flew Gerry Goffin and Carole King out from New York and something happened in the studio. They flew home in the middle of the night—it wasn't gonna work. By this time we're getting closer to the show's air date. Donnie is concerned. The whole time Tommy is pulling on Donnie's shirt sleeve saying, "Donnie, we can do this." Finally, he gave us a shot. I told Donnie, "I've got this band that I work with in clubs called the Candy Store Prophets. We'll rehearse the songs that we would like to record with my group and we'll go in a cheap rehearsal studio and you come down and listen and if you like what you hear, give us the job." He came down and we played him two or three songs and he said, "You guys got it. Go into RCA and start cutting the first album."

-Bobby Hart

The Monkees met us at El Dorado Studios to replace our vocals on the backing tracks we had cut for the pilot. We had a good time jousting around with them. Finally, "Are you ready to try a take?"

They knew the song; they'd heard it on the demo. So Tommy and I went in the booth and we said, "Okay, here comes the track—take one." We played the backing track, and we didn't hear anything. We looked back there and they were all in a dog pile on the floor, wrestling. We stopped and rewound the tape. They got back up on their feet and we said, "Okay, guys, let's try to get this. Bert and Bob really want to have your voices on the recording—Take two!" We looked out, and they were going at it again. We surmised that there was a lot of pent-up energy before they started shooting the show, and they were just getting to know each other. They were four actors, and they were, in a way, trying to outdo each other with their outlandishness. We tried recording for seven takes before we dismissed the session. From that night on, we never had more than one Monkee in the studio at a time. We just didn't trust what might happen.

-Bobby Hart

If you listen to the record of "Gonna Buy Me A Dog," you realize that those guys did not know that this was going to go on the record. They were just rehearsing. You hear at the beginning, Micky says, "Don't mess up the take, Davy" and Davy says, "The take's already messed up, Micky." And it was completely spontaneous. They tried to do it again, but couldn't. Fortunately they had saved the original take. And that was great. That's who we were; that was the great strength of the group, as far as I'm concerned.

-Peter Tork.

When we composed the songs for the pilot show, the TV producers didn't give us any lyrical direction or philosophy or anything. We knew this was going to be the "American Beatles," visually, and we assumed it made the most sense to do a Beatles-influenced sound, but not a rip-off. Actually, "The Monkees" theme was influenced by a Dave Clark Five song called "Catch Us If You Can." That's where we got the finger snapping and "Here we come" opener. Tommy and I wrote that while we were walking down the street on Woodrow Wilson Drive. We were going to the park and when we got that walking beat, we decided that it was a great rhythm to write a song to.

We were almost through producing the first album, and we needed one or two extra songs to complete it. Tommy and I were sitting around writing, and I told him what happened the previous evening. I pulled into my carport and I was flipping the buttons on my radio when I heard for the first time the Beatles' new single, "Paperback Writer." I only heard the fade out, and although they were singing, "Paperback Writer," I heard it as, "Take the last train...," something. Because their song had nothing to do with trains, as I discovered when I heard it again, I thought we should consider writing a train song. We kicked around names of the little towns in Northern Arizona where I used to vacation as a kid, and Clarkdale was one of them. That evolved into "Last Train to Clarksville." The song's about a guy who's going off to war, not knowing if he's ever going to come back. He wants to spend one more night with his girlfriend. We never considered it a war protest song until we heard Micky Dolenz in an interview explaining it that way. I thought, "Why not, it sounds good to me."

-Bobby Hart

P reviously, we had written a song for Paul Revere and the Raiders—"(I'm Not Your) Steppin' Stone." They turned it down. It was one of the hardest sounding records we made with the Monkees. They used to close their concerts with it. After it was a hit for the Monkees, Paul Revere and the Raiders cut it and put it on their album, as did dozens of other acts around the country. One of the most raucous versions I've ever heard was recorded by the Sex Pistols in the 1970's.

"I Wanna Be Free" was one of the few songs that Tommy and I wrote that wasn't commissioned. Tommy heard a Roger Miller song called "One Dyin' and a Buryin'," which is a song about suicide, basically. One of the last lines was "I wanna be free." Tommy

liked it for a title, but was struggling with what the song should be. I came out with the first few lines that took us into the ballad. Later on, when we were asked to write a ballad for *The Monkees* pilot, for Davy walking along the beach musing about his love life, we thought "I Wanna Be Free" would be appropriate, even though it's not a love song. It's kind of a backwards love song. When we recorded it for the album, we asked Don McGuinness, who did many great arrangements for us, to make it into our version of the Beatles' "Yesterday."

-Bobby Hart

We had done American Bandstand on this hayride in Bakersfield. One girl was standing over to the side, and no one was talking to her. So we said, "Why don't you come on the hayride with us?" She said, "Well, no one really talks to me up here." I said, "Rosemary, come on, we'll have a great time."

About two weeks after we got back to Los Angeles, she sent us this unbelievable thank you note. As you opened the card it said in big letters "WORDS." She said, "Tommy and Bobby, WORDS can never express how nice you two were to me at the hayride." I said, "Wow! What a great idea for a song—'Words.'" That was also one of the first times we thought Peter could actually sing on a record. We thought it would be good for him and Micky to sing overlapping vocals.

-Tommy Boyce

Peter and Mike play guitar very well, and Davy clearly was supposed to be the front man, the cute lead singer with maracas and tambourine. So I became the drummer. I'd never played the drums as a professional musician; I'd played rhythm guitar in my previous groups. So, I was being cast as a drummer and I said, "Fine." Like, when ten years before they'd said, "You're a kid in the circus at the turn of the century—here's your elephant." I had no problem with it at all. I was excited about it. I thought it would be great fun. I started practicing immediately and I'm sure they were all curious if I would be able to cut it. And I managed.

-Micky Dolenz

One night after the shooting of the pilot, Micky and I went down to the room where the drums were set up and I taught him to play. Bam-boom-bam. On beat one, do this; on beat two, on beat three, on beat four, real slow. He was doing this in no time flat. I taught him the basics on the snare, on the sock, on the bass, the same thing. The next day, we were lip-synching a dance sequence. They paused to have a script consultation. We turned to the crew and said, "Are these amps live? Can we fire them up?" And we played without ever having played together before. We called off a couple of Chuck Berry tunes.

Michael and I knew the changes on the strings, and Micky counted them off. The extras and the other cast and crew members who didn't have anything to do got up and danced. So right from the start, we could do it. When we went on the road and we needed more musicians than just the three of us, we got Davy a bass. "You just put your fingers here and do this," and he went, "Okay, got it." Just like that. He had it. He knew what he needed to do. He wasn't thinking, "Oh, I can't play." So we were playing together well from the start and we never quit.

-Peter Tork

we'd been rehearsing now for a few months as a band, they set up these instruments in an empty baggage car on this train, and on the way back we were gonna perform for these kids, who didn't know who we were, on songs nobody had heard before, in a train going 80 miles an hour up the coast. So it was, "Take the last train to Clarksville...," and my drums were falling all over—nobody thought to tie the drums down. Because these people were from the television show, they didn't know that you had to tie the drums down or that you had to mike the instruments and our voices. It was very embarrassing.

-Micky Dolenz

W e did a promotion with KHJ, which was the most popular radio station in L.A. They rented a train that went to San Diego and back. The mayor of Del Mar had made it official Monkees Day and turned the town into Clarksville. It was a great promotional idea. They flew us in a helicopter, and we landed on the beach. But, of course, nobody knew who we were yet because the show hadn't aired. All these kids were given this free trip, and we show up on the beach and they go, "Who are you? Where's the free coke? Where are the hot dogs?" Because

was distraught. I look back on it now, and it makes all kinds of sense that we didn't play. Obviously, we didn't know enough about pop music record production to be able to crank out two tunes a week for the show, as well as act in it. When we started filming the TV episodes, it took us five twelve-hour days per week. We'd walk out of those things with our eyes crossed, and we were in no condition to be making records. We finally did make our *Headquarters* album. We were doing forty to fifty and sometimes seventy takes apiece on the basic tracks. I didn't realize beforehand, but we weren't ready. But I was upset that I wasn't playing on the tracks on the first album. I did play fourth chair guitar on the two sessions that Mike produced. So that's me on "Papa Gene's Blues." You can't hear me, but I'm in there; four guitars all playing the same thing.

I was raised in the Pete Seeger folk singing tradition of authenticity, integrity and honor. I thought bands played on their records. So when they told us to show up for our first recording session, I brought my guitar. They didn't want me to play. They said, "What are you complaining about? You're making money." I

-Peter Tork

James Frawley and Bob Rafelson

In the first show I directed, "Royal Flash," our edit exceeded the time limit by a few minutes. Because of our time crunch, I spent thirty-two hours straight in the editing room cutting the show down. When we finished, we were frustrated to find ourselves a minute-and-a-half under. Well, we weren't going to go back and figure out what we wanted to add back in, so we decided to shoot the Monkees improvising to shtick at the end of the program. It became so popular, it became a part of the style of the show.

-James Frawley

I do think some of the cutting and breaking of the fourth wall that we often got credit for was done more out of necessity. There were certainly times when I'm editing the show and it doesn't go together; the guy walks out the door and the next scene he's already in the room and there's no transition. You're trying to get the thing done and you say, "Screw it, just cut to him there." And so a lot of the jump cuts and the flashiness of the show was out of necessity. We didn't have the film to cover it right. So we were getting credit for doing something that we had no choice but to do.

-Ward Sylvester

Jim Frawley was very nurturing. He provided a lot of help for me to learn acting. He created a safe haven and made it okay to be silly, which I didn't need too much encouragement to do.

-Mike Nesmith

David's dressing room was traditional Broadway. He had a huge mirror with lights all around, and postcards and letters and photos from well wishers—right off of Broadway. He had a bunk bed and a filing cabinet. He could look at himself in the mirror twenty-four hours a day, when he wasn't on the set. Peter's was very bohemian, and loaded with musical instruments. It was banks of pianos and guitars and basses and music and instruments and tools and amps and ear phones, and you could hardly get in there. You just kind of crawled in and managed to just get behind this mass of electronic stuff. Mike's was the strangest. It was a psychedelic, black-light, Andy Warhol kind of pit of lights and strange colors. There were a lot of safety pins around from wardrobe and he just stuck about a thousand in one wall. I asked him about it and he just said, "Well, you know, I just kind of like it." It was a psychedelic experience, not what you'd expect from Mike. And magazines about motorcycles and trucks in the midst of all this psychedelia. That was the counterpoint. Mine was very simple; shag carpet, a candle and four pillows—that was it. That was my little womb.

-Micky Dolenz

We all had our own dressing room trailers. I decorated mine with cigarette wrappers. This was back in the days when it was okay to smoke. I would pick up cigarette wrappers that I would find lying around, and, as time went on, I had this entire wall of cigarette wrappers stapled to the wall, and it gave it a really interesting texture. Cigarette packages are cool-looking anyway and then they had this shiny side of it—the cellophane it was wrapped in.

There was a place in Texas that I frequented when I was in college which was just a little hole-in-the-wall called Hip's Bubble Room. It was lighted primarily by the kind of bubble lights that you put on Christmas trees. So I had lit my own dressing room with bubble lights. I bought a bunch and strung them up. So between the cigarette wrappers and the bubble lights, I hung there most of the time, and enjoyed it.

-Mike Nesmith

The show had gone on the air in September of 1966. I hadn't been out of the house or off the set in a few months. It was Christmas, and I was going out shopping to the same old shopping center I'd shopped at all my life as a kid in the San Fernando Valley. I had a couple of days off for Christmas, and I was going up north to see my family and I went to buy presents. I ran into this shopping center. I'm going down my list to see what I want to buy first. All of a sudden I hear screams, and people start running at me, and I thought there was a fire. I turned and I ran outside through these big double doors, and I look back and they're still coming at me. I suddenly realize that they recognize me! They were coming after me. I became angry. I had to leave. I had to send somebody later to do my shopping. That's the first time I realized how successful the show had been.

-Micky Dolenz

The Monkees was like this little nuclear reaction that they'd started, by their own design. You get these four characters in the same place at the same time, and then let them go. You have to contain it or else it burns a hole through the center of the Earth, but if you contain it too much, it goes out. So they had to constantly maintain this balance between absolutely insanity, and crushing it and breaking our spirit, because that wouldn't have worked either. One of the reasons that the show was so successful was because they were able to capture our energy and spirit.

THE
PRESSURE COOKER

-Micky Dolenz

In those days we filmed the show on thirty-five millimeter film. It was very time-consuming, because only a single camera was used. Now, a sitcom can be shot with five cameras in front of a live audience on a Friday night. In those days, they would come in on Monday, read the script and then shoot laboriously every day from seven in the morning to seven at night, one little bit at a time; move the camera and do it again. They would do that all day. They would record or do whatever merchandising work there was to do at night and go off on the weekends and do concerts. It was a pressure cooker that was exacerbated by the fact that we had put together four guys who had almost nothing in common. They had no shared backgrounds, shared interests or shared experiences,

which made it very difficult.

The show required two new songs every week, one for what we called romps which, in my view, were the first music videos; and the other, a performance piece. It's a tremendous pressure to produce a weekly television show, but worse in those days because of the three days it took to shoot, and the fact that you did twenty-eight episodes a year. It was a constant struggle when I was producing the show. I would be working on scripts in various stages of development for the next six or eight shows; anything from hearing ideas to trying to polish the script for next week's show. We would be shooting twelve hours a day on the stage, preparing next week's show in terms of casting and wardrobe and sets and budgets. The last three or four weeks of shows were in various stages of editing and

post-production, all of which was very cumbersome. It was being done at a film studio, so the show had to be scored reel by reel and if you didn't like a sound effect, you went back and did the whole reel over again. So, we were under enormous pressure to get the show on the air. We had to get the show to New York by one p.m. Monday afternoon to air that night. There were deliveries that were so tight, that if there had been a snow storm in New York and the plane had been diverted, the show would not have gotten on the air. So everyone was screaming. It seems trivial in retrospect, but in those days, missing your air date was catastrophic.

-*Ward Sylvester*

Success changes everything. Davy Jones once drove right through the gate at Screen Gems because the guard didn't recognize him. He knocked it right down. Now, anybody else would say "Okay, he's suspended. He's banned." They couldn't do that with our group. We knew how to talk to the guys. And the next day, I smashed the gate open. There was very little distance in our behavior, except I was more premeditated and calculated.

-Bob Rafelson

We weren't encouraged to memorize the scripts. As long as we knew where the scenes were going, what plot points we had to establish, what exposition we had to come up with, then we just rambled it. When other, experienced actors were around, it was difficult for them because they were not used to our insanity and improvisational style. Hans Conried, a marvelous actor, guested on the show. I was a big fan of his and excited to be working with him. Halfway through his second day, he blew up: "I can't stand these kids!" He was furious. He just couldn't deal with this total informal insanity; that we were running around the set and up the rafters and re-writing—it was crazy! I was very embarrassed. But that's what they were trying to capture. And they did. Nobody's been able to do it since.

-Micky Dolenz

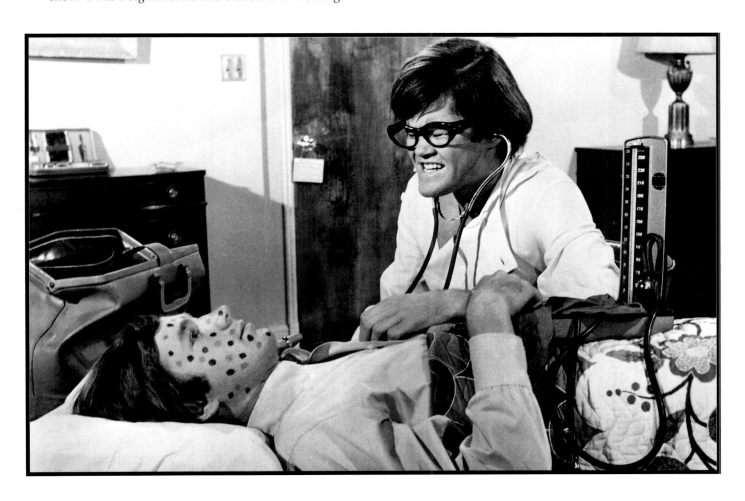

We were all jealous that the Monkees were making it because we thought they broke the rules. We thought there was a book of rules that said you had to get a guitar, a pair of Beatle boots and some unique clothes. You have to go in a van for three years and you have to rehearse every day and not have a day job and then you become brothers. The Monkees broke all the rules. They even had a wardrobe person choosing clothes for them. There's always some sort of jealousy when somebody comes along and steals your business and then becomes successful at it. You've got to figure the Hollies were saying, "This is not quite fair—they're doing my business there." And I would say, "My God, they've even got an English guy with the same accent as me. He's doing Herman better than Herman does it."

-Peter Noone

The producers wanted to see if we could perform music in front of an audience. They had Dick Clark book us in Hawaii, so that if we were lousy, no one would know—it's all those miles across the sea. Not only did we go to Hawaii for our first concert, but we played at the Miss Teenage American Beauty Pageant, which had an audience already built-in. We didn't have to sell tickets. I think we played half a dozen tunes, including "I'm A Believer," "Last Train to Clarksville," and "I Wanna Be Free." And they went crazy. The record that was number one in Hawaii was not "Last Train to Clarksville" but the B side, "Take A Giant Step." Because there were no trains in Hawaii, they turned the record over. We all hung out in a hotel and we met some interesting people, including Yevgeny Yevtushenko, a Russian poet, who was there as the funny man in the entourage. I met my first wife there.

-Davy Jones

I'M A BELIEVER

I supervised the first two albums, both of which went to Number One—*The Monkees* and *More Of The Monkees*. The individual song that was near and dearest to my heart was "I'm A Believer," because Neil Diamond really wanted to keep the song for himself, and it was a major fight to get it from him. I think it's Neil's biggest song as a writer. It's my particular favorite because that song catapulted the Monkees into a whole different level, and got the whole feeling of every boy and girl in America wanting to be part of the Monkees phenomenon.

-Don Kirshner

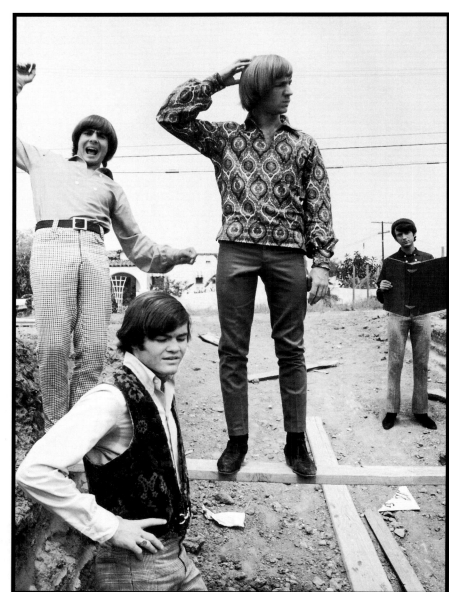

I flew out to Los Angeles from New York with the backing track of "I'm a Believer." They hadn't heard it yet, and it was either myself or Neil Diamond singing out in front so they could learn the song. All the guys were there. Mike Nesmith, as I recall, came with a girlfriend—looked like she was about fourteen. He had a bad attitude right from the beginning, and I didn't know why. I played the record and everybody was politely accepting of it and thought it was good, and he had no comment. Finally he said, "I'm a producer too, and that isn't a hit." And I was obviously embarrassed, so I thought I'd break the awkward silence with a joke. I said, "You have to picture it with strings and horns." Now it was obvious we weren't gonna put a big string section and horns on that record, but he thought I was serious and he said, "Well, maybe with strings and horns...." Everybody broke up and it was really embarrassing. He got so angry, our relationship went downhill from there. I'm sure glad it turned out to be Record of the Year. Mike and I never hit it off, which is unfortunate, because I had a great time with the other guys in the studio.

-Jeff Barry

Jeff Barry produced "Your Auntie Grizelda." He was a pretty good producer. He said, "Make some sound effects here in the middle." "Oh, no, I can't do that." So I tried and I got into the swing of it and I started to lose my tempo, but it was funny. Jack Keller co-wrote it. He said, "We got a song for you Peter, it's a protest song, like '19th Nervous Breakdown.'"

-Peter Tork

The second record was so angering, because Donnie almost militantly cut us out of the process. By that time we were playing our own music onstage, and we were righteously pissed that the album was released without our knowing anything at all about it. We thought those tracks were being recorded for the TV show, not a new album. We were on the road at the time, and somebody went across the street to the mall to get a copy. We had to buy the album just to hear it.

-Peter Tork

DON KIRSHNER

In the context of the show's tight production schedule, we relied upon the Kirshner music machine, a very successful, largely songwriting but also song-producing organization based in New York. Donnie Kirshner was the man with the golden ears. He had developed a stable of very successful songwriters, principally Gerry Goffin and Carole King and Barry Mann and Cynthia Weil. So I thought, "This is a wonderful resource." And there really wasn't any thought that this would be a problem. When the first

criticism started coming through that the Monkees weren't really a group, it seemed bizarre to me that anybody would think they were. It's like somebody saying, "Do you understand that Barbara Eden doesn't sleep in a bottle at night?" Of course she doesn't, she's an actress playing a part on television; she's not a genie. We lacked the foresight that the guys would start to feel that "That's supposed to be us singing and playing and not only is it not, but it's not something we might want to play or sing." I think Kirshner exacerbated it. There were a couple reasons why it got worse. Kirshner would not fly, so he didn't want to leave New York. He was always the eminence back in New York who would be mailing things to Los Angeles. Secondly, he had a great taste for personal publicity. He wanted the credit for the Monkees. Now, he certainly deserved it at the beginning. I mean, Tommy Boyce and Bobby Hart were songwriters he worked with and he helped them pick the music that they produced on the first album. But he wanted the world to know it was him, and it came out as if, "Those four kids on the screen really don't have anything to do with it," which was really hard on us. I think there was also a lack of respect from Kirshner. He was not dealing with them on a daily basis so it was like, "Oh, well, they're just those four kids on the show and any four kids would do."

They also were traveling in more music than television circles because there weren't many television stars their age in those days, and their interests were more bohemian. The happening scene in Hollywood then was a music scene; now it's a feature film scene. Then, the hip twenty-five-year-olds with the money and the Jaguars were in the music business. So those were the peers and the contemporaries that the Monkees would see socially. And they would see the Monkees as musicians. It became very uncomfortable, particularly for Mike, who took his own music very seriously, and for Peter, who had been a musical performer. I don't think at the beginning David much cared. I mean, he didn't need for anyone to think he had written "Consider Yourself" when he sang it on Broadway, and Micky saw himself more as an actor. But the cumulative weight of it quickly became intolerable, and they wanted to do their own music.

-Ward Sylvester

Kirshner's focus was on the music and it was "whatever it takes to have hits" and that was always what he was interested in. He would hear a song and he would get really excited and he would go, "Monster, monster, it's a monster!" That was his word for it. And I think he was more right than wrong. If you asked him to rhyme heart, he would probably not be able to come up with a rhyme and he certainly can't dance or put two notes in a row but boy, you play it for him and it's what they call "ears." And he certainly had ears.

-Jeff Barry

I didn't even know who Don Kirshner was. I remember seeing him around, but I thought he was somebody's assistant. He was very quiet, he didn't say anything. I'd never been introduced to him like, "This is Don Kirshner from New York—you gotta listen to what he says." I mean, that's not the kind of thing you said to the four of us anyway. Because we were pretty unruly. We were recording and he was throwing in his two cents. Peter, I think, was trying to get some kind of bass groove. Donnie said something about, "It needs a couple more db's on the high end" or something that I thought was an inane comment. By now, we'd been there for twelve hours and I had an empty cup of coke I'd been sipping—there was just ice left—and so I just went and flipped it upside down on the top of his head like a little cone. "Oh, Donnie, be quiet." And everybody laughed—"Ha, ha, ha, hah—Monkee pranks," you know? Which is what it was. We were always on. To this day, you get the four of us in a room, you open an ice box and the light goes on, and we'll do twenty minutes. Donnie didn't find that as funny as everybody else. He took me aside and he was very diplomatic about it and I wasn't offended. He said, "You know, I have to maintain a degree of respect here." And I was like, "Why? Who are you?" I had no idea. Maybe I'd been told, but I was busy building my gyrocopter in the basement.

-Micky Dolenz

I learned a lot from Donnie Kirshner. He was very meticulous and organized; he was constantly making notes. He always had lists and formulas. For instance, "Valleri"—he wanted a song with a girl's name in the title. That was part of the formula that he wanted on the next album. He was flamboyant: limousines, hundred dollar tips for the drivers and the engineers in the studio. We didn't spend a lot of time with him. Tommy and I mostly saw him in New York. He was our boss in the organizational structure, but we worked more closely with Lester Sill. Lester was a great guy, a father figure to us. When we came to Los Angeles, he took us into his family, nurtured us as creators and gave us the freedom to develop.

-Bobby Hart

I was home one day in New Jersey, and a van pulled up with a huge color portrait of the Monkees. Davy Jones wrote, "From one nice Jewish boy to another," and all the boys inscribed it. It was emotionally very important to me because it was the first real sign that they really cared for me and respected my contribution.

The incident when Mike Nesmith put his fist through the wall at the Beverly Hills Hotel is very vivid. I hated to fly in those days, but I had flown out to give each boy a quarter of a million dollars. It's a lot of money today—and in those days it was even more. That was mostly from royalties on the first album. I also had under my arm a song called "Sugar, Sugar," which I wanted them to do after "A Little Bit Me, A Little Bit You." With me at the Beverly Hills Hotel was my wife, Sheila, and my mother-in-law, Joyce, and we thought we were gonna celebrate. Mike had given me a lot of heat that he didn't like the records. He wanted to do it his way. It was a little disconcerting to me because we were so successful. I handed each boy—Mike, Peter, Davy and Micky—his check. If they had problems with the records, I would have respected them if they hadn't taken the money. They all took the money, and Mike proceeded to put his hand through the wall at the Beverly Hills Hotel, which amazed me because I thought they were pretty solid walls. He said, "We're not recording for you anymore. We want to do our own thing." But they all

took the money on the work we did on the first albums, then went crying back to Bert and Bob. Because Bert's father was the president of Columbia Pictures, he had a lot of clout. He said, "We want to get rid of Donnie Kirshner."

-Don Kirshner

Don Kirshner's sidekick, Herb Moelis, wagged the contract at me and said, "We've got a contract and this is the contract that you've got." And I smashed my fist into the wall and I said, "Yeah, well, that could have been your face." I just lost my temper for a few seconds. What a schlemiel this guy was. Herbie.

-Mike Nesmith

What we asked for was to be allowed to be the studio musicians on our own records. We did not ask for creative control. We did not ask to be the producers. We did not ask to replace Kirshner. Kirshner, whose idea of control is "everything in place!" saw this as the Barbarians at the gates of the Holy Roman Empire, and he wasn't having any of it. Bert, who had some pull with Columbia Pictures, went up the chain of command over the top and down the other side and the order came from Bob to Kirshner. "The next single must have the boys themselves being the musicians on the B-side." So Donnie put out a record where professional studio musicians had done both sides. He released the record in Canada. Fired, bam! Just like that. I think they were getting sick of him for reasons of their own.

-Peter Tork

The song, "A Little Bit Me, A Little Bit You," which Neil Diamond wrote, was the reason I got fired at Columbia Pictures. It was an amazing year; I had published the Academy Award-winning song, "Born Free," and the Monkees were outselling the Beatles. I had promised Neil Diamond—and in the music business, your word is your bond—that if the record "I'm A Believer" went to Number One I would give him the follow-up. At that time, I got a call from Abe Schneider and Bert Schneider and they said to me, "The boys wanna do their own thing." I said, "There's no way; I've got a contract giving me creative control. I've committed to Neil Diamond for the follow-up record, and unless you can't whistle or hum it, he's gonna get it." I thought "A Little Bit Me, A Little Bit You" was rather ordinary for Neil. It reminded me of his old song, "Cherry, Cherry." But I had to keep my word to Neil. I put it out, and then I got fired. Prior to the Monkees, I had sold my business to Columbia Pictures and formed a new, ten-year deal with them. When I was twenty-nine years old, the first check I got was a million-eight. I was making five times more than the president of Columbia Pictures, so they got rid of me.

-Don Kirshner

HEADQUARTERS

When I was playing bass with the Turtles, I had the opportunity to arrange the brass and vocal parts on their hit recording of "Happy Together." It started climbing the charts, and it was just a matter of a month or two when Michael Nesmith approached me at a Turtles performance at the Whiskey-A-Go-Go and said, "We want a new record producer and I've elected you." I couldn't believe it. I wasn't sure I could actually produce. He said he would teach me everything I'd need to know. "Trust me," he said, "you'll be making six figures in six weeks." I told him I'd take a shot at it. I had to leave the Turtles, which was disappointing; I was having a lot of fun and I'd only been with them a number of months. Touring with them was one of the great times of my life.

-Chip Douglas

Every record we put out was selling millions of copies. They were backing trucks up to record stores, unloading the trucks and the things would vanish into a sea of locusts. Being able to sit in a studio and play music and know that it was going to have that kind of effect, that's a real interesting place to work from. And you don't get to do that very often. You know, we'd play this one little song and it's gonna go out and five million people are gonna buy it, and another forty million people are gonna hear it. It tends to make you giddy, but it's also unsustainable. It's like taking a ride in the vomit comet, and you're coming

over the top and you're gonna get a minute of weightlessness, so enjoy it. Because when you come down, you're gonna pull the G's and end up sitting on the passenger side.

-Mike Nesmith

The premise of *Headquarters* was for them to be really the Monkees and play all of the instruments. I wanted to have a four-piece band going somehow, and Micky played drums and Michael played guitar. Peter was a bass player too, and a good one, but he kept playing the piano in the studio and I thought, "It's good we have him on keyboards, but we don't have a bass player, so I guess I'll have to do it." I was playing a lot of bass in those days and I figured, "Well, this might be a way to hold it together," because we needed someone and we couldn't get an outside musician. Bert Schneider advised me not to. He said, "Get somebody else," and I said, "We can't, we have to keep it within the family." So I played the bass and we did our tracks in that manner.

-Chip Douglas

The harpsichord was something I wanted to do because I am partly a classicist. Bach was my favorite composer, and harpsichords were my thing. When Mike was in my dressing room, I was noodling around with the solo for "The Girl I Knew Somewhere," and I hit that discord on the down beat at the end—I hadn't meant to do that. I said, "What was that?" Mike said, "I heard it!" That was great—we were tickled to death to have this funny note on the record. On "Shades of Grey," Mike wrote the horn and cello parts, sang them to me, and I notated them. I was also really pleased with that little piano introduction I wrote. We were just thrilled to death with that song.

-Peter Tork

"No Time" started out as a jam. Then Mike and I went into the control booth and wrote the lyrics. "Hobber reeber sabosoven" is Bill Cosby. "Running from the rising heat to find a place to hide" is about police and marijuana, and "Andy you're a dandy, you don't seem to make no sense" is about Andy Warhol.

-Micky Dolenz

The sessions for *Headquarters* were rough at first, because they weren't used to being in the studio recording as a band. Micky had a lot of energy on the drums, but his tempo was up and down. I had to edit a number of the takes together to make good steady ones. "Randy Scouse Git" is one of the most unusual songs on the *Headquarters* album. When we were recording it, I thought Micky was nuts. "You can't have this kettle drum and do all of this weird stuff here." He wanted this kettle drum to rise up from nowhere at the end. He had it all pictured exactly how he wanted it.

-Chip Douglas

The recording sessions for *Headquarters* were wonderful. I remember them better than any of the other sessions, because it was just the four of us and we were determined to play every note on every track. We had a marvelous producer with Chip Douglas, and some great songs. We recorded Harry Nilsson's first tune, "Cuddly Toy." That's where we met Harry, and I became very close friends with him. He was working at a bank, in the check clearance department, and writing songs on the side. He brought a couple of songs to Lester Sill at Screen Gems Music Publishing. Harry told me later that Lester said, "You can quit the bank now, Harry."

-*Micky Dolenz*

We were in Studio C at RCA, which is a small room. One day, Micky came in with some tempera paints and started painting the glass between the control room and the studio. This went on for weeks. Everybody joined in and we ended up with this incredible piece of artwork.

The night we finished *Headquarters*, the president of RCA was coming down with a bunch of guys to hear the album. My boss came down beforehand, looked at the room, and said, "It's a mess." I said, "Just leave it alone, the guys want the painting on the wall—they haven't taken any pictures of it yet." He said, "OK, we'll try and do that." When we walked in at five that evening, the place was spotless, and the glass had been washed off. The Monkees lost it and freaked. The president of RCA had to take all this abuse, merely because someone had washed the glass off!

-Hank Cicalo

"No Time" was in a Chuck Berry style. We assigned the writing credit to Hank Cicalo, who got into trouble, because engineers were not supposed to solicit songs, which is what RCA thought he had done. We had to explain to them that it was a tip. He bought a house with the money.

--Peter Tork

IN CONCERT

We would burst out of these big, mock Vox speakers onto the stage and the place would go bananas. We had one of the first multimedia presentations; we projected this film up behind us on a big movie screen. We'd play big arenas and it was just when the little flash cameras had come out on the market, the instamatics, with a flashcube. So like 15,000 times four of these little flash cubes would go off simultaneously. I get up behind the drums and I couldn't hear any count so Mike would turn and he would look at me and I'd look at him and we'd all look at each other because you couldn't hear or see a thing. They didn't have monitors in those days. And so he would go, "One, two, three, four...," and we started with "Clarksville." And I never even heard that much, just my drums. Mike would have to keep tapping his foot; I've seen pictures and videos of me in concert looking at Mike's foot.

-Micky Dolenz

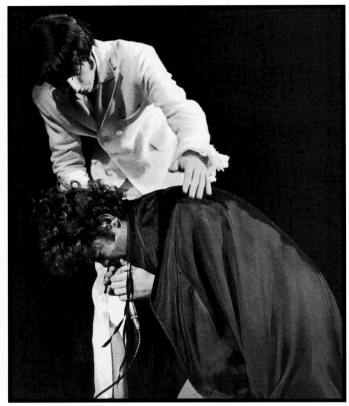

Always before a Monkees concert, we would have a group hug and then we'd run to our marks. They would play "The Monkees" theme on tape. "Here we come, walking down the street..." And then we did "Clarksville," "Steppin' Stone," "I'm a Believer" and "Mary, Mary." During "Mary, Mary," everybody would leave the stage and Micky would go, "Mary, Mary, Mary, Mary...." And then we would do our solo numbers. I played "Cripple Creek" on banjo. The back-up band came out and Mike sang "You Can't Judge a Book by Looking at the Cover." Davy sang

"Gonna Build a Mountain." And Micky did "I Got a Woman," sort of a cross between Ray Charles and James Brown, copying his cape routine. Micky would somersault, and the first couple of times he banged his knees so bad that he had to wear foam pads. He would sing, "I can't stop now, I can't stop now." When we played the Hollywood Bowl there was a pool in front of the stage. Micky took a flying somersault and landed in the pool.

-Peter Tork

I got a call from Ward Sylvester. "You wanna take your band out and open for the Monkees, and back them on their solo numbers?" I said sure. They were quick gigs, often one city each night for twelve or fourteen nights. The pandemonium of the fans was astounding, and there were times when you were actually fearing for your life. I remember being trapped in stairwells where the fans had gotten by the guard and filled up these small areas where you were pressed against the wall and you didn't know if you were going to be able to breathe. There were scary times having clothes torn and ripped and there were great fun times, too. In Toronto, I remember landing on the airport runway, rather than going to the terminal. Limos pulled right up and we were escorted by the police. In rush hour traffic, these motorcycle patrolmen pulled all the cars off the interstates and let our limos pass freely to the hotel.

-Bobby Hart

We played at the Maple Leaf Garden, which is a giant stadium. At every juncture they would have nurses, with big trays stacked with wet towels. Whenever they saw a little girl looking like she was a little too overcome, and of course, that was most of them, they would take wet towels and plop them in their face and cool them down. It was fascinating to look at from the stage perspective and see the stuff that was being hurled toward the stage, and hear the constant roar of screaming. We could have been playing or not playing, no one would have noticed. It was total pandemonium.

-Bobby Hart

I remember once in New York we pulled away from a hotel, and the police and the guards hadn't been able to keep the kids away from the limo. A couple of them grabbed onto the back and hung onto the antenna or the roof and the driver was told to take off. He's in the front and the window between us and him is up, and he's going thirty miles an hour down Fifth Avenue and these kids are hanging on the back of the car going, "No, wait, stop...." We didn't know what to do. He took a corner at thirty miles an hour and these two kids just bounced off. They got up and were okay, and had a great story to tell. It got kind of scary at times.

-Micky Dolenz

We were staying at the Hotel Warwick which, by that time, was the only hotel who'd have us in New York. In other hotels, we would usually sneak the Monkees through the service or garbage entrance, or sometimes through a tunnel that came up in an office building across the street. The Warwick was utterly unsuited for that; it was on a corner with streets running in both directions, with no way out except through the lobby.

By that time, we were carrying our own security chief, whom we found in Phoenix. He had been a policeman, and had been extremely good at coordination. The only way we could get the guys out of the hotel was to have security men link arms on both sides of a gauntlet that ran from the elevator through the lobby to the curb, and we could run down the middle of that and tumble into the limousine. That was our plan.

The fans knew we had to leave for the concert. There

was no other way to deal with it. Now, our security chief controlled the elevators with a key, and he stopped them all. I rounded up all four of the guys, and we got in. The doors opened and we ran through the gauntlet and tumbled into the back of the car. As usual, the four boys and I are in the back and the security chief is riding shotgun. The driver isn't moving and the kids are starting to climb all over the car. The security chief is yelling at the driver, "Move, move, get out of here!" The driver turns around and says, "Does Mr. Water know you're using his car?" We'd gotten in the wrong limousine.

-Ward Sylvester

I remember very well seeing the Monkees live for the first time. It was in San Francisco, at the Cow Palace, and I was sitting next to Bert Schneider. He was looking around at the audience, not quite believing what he had created; it scared him. "Look at these kids—they're going nuts." And they really were. They were screaming, they were hysterical. The Monkees had it all choreographed very carefully. Mike came out, waving two maracas in each hand, and drove them all wild. There were costume changes. It was really a great show, and I was quite impressed by the way they were playing on stage, as opposed to in the studio, where it was much harder for them. On stage, they just let loose and gave it their all.

-Chip Douglas

We had been playing at the arena level, and the sound systems were the half time sound systems they used at basketball games. So when we went in there, we had to carry our sound system with us. Well, you walk into Detroit Olympia Stadium

and 19,000 fourteen-year-old girls torch off like that, nobody hears anything for days. So we got to playing louder and louder, and by the time we played together a few months on the road, we could play really loud— but I don't know how good we ever actually played. We had lots of good times.

-Mike Nesmith

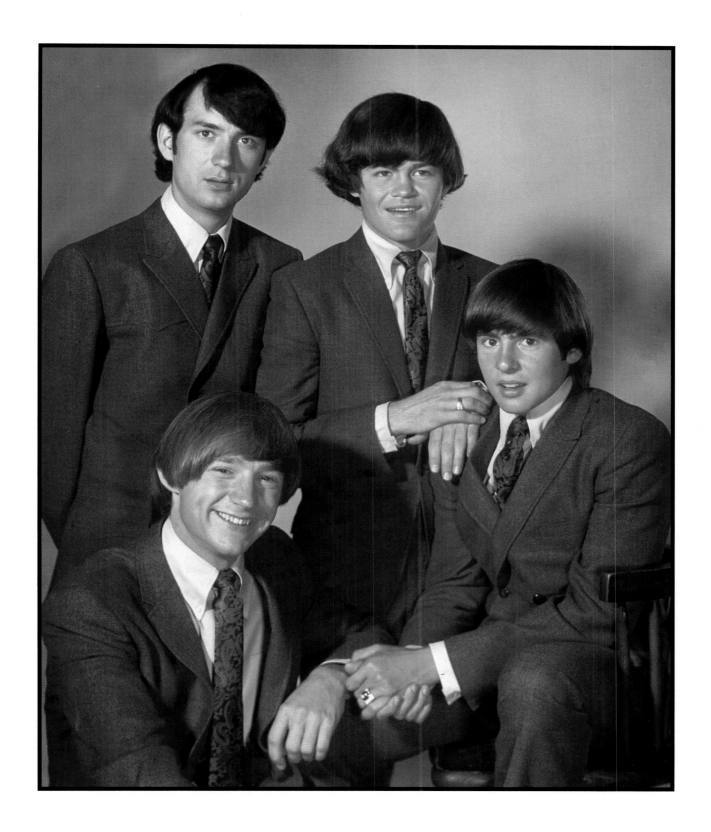

I was performing a song from *Oliver!* on *The Ed Sullivan Show* when the Beatles made their American debut. I saw this amazing reaction and I thought, "I want a bit of this—this is good."

I remember getting into the lift with Ringo Starr. I was always a cheeky little guy. He had a cold at the time and I remember saying, "Let me blow your nose for you, I'm closer than you are." Ringo said, "I know."

-Davy Jones

I was protecting myself by not becoming too involved, because I always feared that what I wanted would be taken away from me, so I didn't dare want anything.

When Micky said, "You can't go back in the studio," that was the end for me of any hopes of having a real live group, which is what I wanted at the time. At that point, I had had it. I was utterly disappointed. So when I had the chance, I quit.

-Peter Tork

Mike Nesmith walked in for his audition, and he had a bag of laundry over his shoulder. He had his pants tucked into his boots, which came up to about his knees. He had his wool hat on, even though it was the middle of summer. I thought, "This guy's just come out of the mountains. What's going on here?" So he came in and said, "I don't have much time. How long is this gonna take?" And I thought, "Oh, we got a rare one here." He was on Colpix Records; that's why he was brought in. He never sat down; he just stood there. He was going to do his laundry.

-Davy Jones

Remember John Wayne's shirt in *Stagecoach*? He wore a double-breasted, windbreaker front. I thought it was a great looking shirt. Our head of wardrobe, Gene Ashman, worked up a variation for us. What I wanted was to be John Wayne—not just wear his shirt. But I got the shirt, so that wasn't bad.

-Mike Nesmith

I think all the fellow musicians that were in L.A. at the time, like Love, the Byrds and the Buffalo Springfield, all loved the Monkees and thought they were great. Everybody loved their TV show and loved them as singers. I think it was mostly the people who weren't making it as successful musicians who were more critical of them, and it was the press. They had a lot of friends in the Los Angeles music scene, I remember.

-Chip Douglas

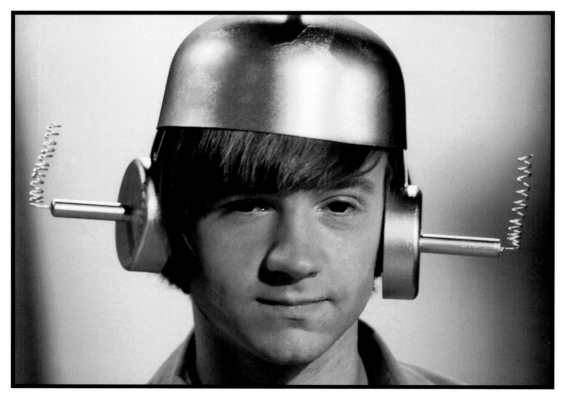

The weight and speed and the gush of attention is inhuman. It is beyond the capacity of anybody to absorb. It's one thing for a banker to work his way up to the point where he's making hundreds of thousands of dollars a year. It's another thing to make a million-five in two years after having lived on $50 a week.

-Peter Tork

"Randy Scouse Git," or, as it was known in England, "Alternative Title," was a song I free associated about my experiences in England. There are references to the Beatles, "the four kings of EMI," to Mama Cass, to Samantha, the woman who was gonna become my first wife, to a roadie and his birthday, and to a girl who had shown up a couple of days before and was hanging around. I was watching a television show, *'Til Death Do Us Part*, that was later rewritten for America as *All In The Family*. The Archie Bunker character, played by Alf Garnet, called his son-in-law, the Meathead character, a randy scouse git. I thought

that was hilarious, even though I didn't know what it meant. I found out later that it was slang for horny Liverpudlian idiot. "Randy" in England is horny; "scouse" is a person from Liverpool, and a "git" is a jerk. In America the record company didn't release a single from *Headquarters*, but in Europe they wanted this one. But they said, "You can't use those words." I said, "Why?" and that's when they explained to me what it meant. I said, "Well, that's ridiculous. What do I have to do?" "Come up with an 'alternative title.'" Ta-da! Simple as that. Boring but effective.

-Micky Dolenz

The first record I ever bought was "Poetry in Motion" by Johnny Tillotson; I didn't even have a record player and I bought it. I was about twelve years old, and I used to sing songs like "Donna" by Ritchie Valens, and songs by Buddy Holly, with my sister in hospitals and old folks homes. They'd ask, "What about the little guy who sings those Buddy Holly songs?" In between Elvis and the Beatles, there were all these pretty boys with the ties and the slicked back hair, teenage idols like Fabian, Frankie Avalon and Bobby Rydell—those were my influences.

-Davy Jones

As we got to know each other, we would get together on Sundays at Hazeltine Park in the Valley and have a baseball game.

Peter would show up with his entourage and they all looked like flower power; it was like they were skipping around the maypole all the time. Then you've got Micky with his family, and then I'd be there with my girlfriend or, later, my wife. We'd have a great time, and then we'd all go back to Micky's or Peter's house and swim in the pool. Michael never joined us.

He was never, ever part of that little team. At our first Christmas when we'd been filming, I bought them all a portable, color TV for their dressing room. I liked to give presents—it was a nice thing to do. They all thanked me very much. I'm leaving the studio that night, and there's our makeup man with a TV under his arm, the one I'd given to Mike. He gave it to the makeup man! Kind of weird. It was a nice gesture on his part, but you know....

-Davy Jones

I believe thirty years from now they'll still be showing *The Monkees*, as they did the Marx Brothers and the Dead End Kids and the Bowery Boys and the Three Stooges and I'm not joking; I really think they will be.

-Davy Jones

I like, respect and love each of the guys in different proportions. Somehow or other, though, Jonesy got my heart. I don't know why, because I don't like him very much. Sometimes he's great to hang with and sometimes he's very difficult, which is not so true of the other two. Michael is deserving of an enormous amount of respect, as far as I'm concerned; he's a man of extraordinary accomplishment. And Micky's very easy to hang with. We get into flights of political discussions and we talk about subatomic physics, to the extent that either of us know anything about it. He's great to talk to. I have a lot of fun with him and always have.

-Peter Tork

We used to fight like brothers. Peter decked me once. I had seven stitches put in my eye. I came back and gave him the bill. That's when it only cost $75 to have that done. But all in all, I think I'd do anything for any one of them. I'd do anything I had to to help in any way I could, because once you've bonded and you've had this thing such as the Monkees, to me, a friend is a friend for life. But this was more. This was finding three brothers I never had.

-Davy Jones

In Australia there was an extraordinarily cute fan climbing a tree outside my hotel window. I was really quite fetched with her. She really loved me—I was the one. And we were leaving. We all got into the limo, and we started to drive away and she started to run after us. And the other guys were saying, "Pick her up—go ahead, take her to the airport," and I couldn't do it. I just waved goodbye and

she went, "Ahhhh...." I kind of wish I had. There was really something special there.

-Peter Tork

LONDON

I went to London to run away from the Don Kirshner confrontation. I was supposed to be at a recording session in New York, but I hopped a plane to London. We were supposed to be there in a few weeks. Somebody set it up for me to meet Paul McCartney, and that was gonna be the big Monkee-Beatle meeting. I brought my autograph book; I never got the autograph, but I wanted to. He was very gracious and treated me like a peer, which I appreciated. And we just had a great chat and I was thrilled, just absolutely thrilled. And I loved it and had a wonderful time. Mike showed up a week or so later and we did *Top of the Pops*. That's where I met Samantha Juste, and we eventually got married. After we were all there, the Beatles threw us a big party.

-Micky Dolenz

I was invited to a recording session. So I dressed up in all my caftans and beads and glasses with sparkle stuff, and I was sure I was gonna go into this unbelievable pop-historical-Andy-Warholesque-Fellini event with the Beatles and groupies and God knows what. I walk into EMI Recording Studios on Abbey Road and it's like a doctor's office—bright fluorescent lights. The guys are sitting there in shirts and t-shirts and slacks with their instruments, and George Martin is in the booth. "Right, once again, and three, four...." I was so stoned and stunned. I was just walking around, "Ohhhh." "Right, okay, once again.... Right, cut it, time for tea, lads." And the guy comes in with a big tray of tea and sits it on this card table and they all sit around and we had tea for twenty minutes. And I'm blown away. I just couldn't believe it. And then they went right back to work; they were working lads from the north. They just did this sixteen hours a day for years. That's where all that stuff came from. So I floated out about an hour later.

-Micky Dolenz

I was staying with John Lennon during the recording of the *Sgt. Pepper* album. He would come home and play the acetates from the day's sessions. "What do you think of that sound? Do you think there's too much bass on there?" And of course I just didn't have any way to talk to him because he was just rearranging my musical realities at the time. I said, "This is just miraculous. This is some of the most innovative and creative and interesting stuff I've ever heard." And he showed me a picture of the album cover. So when he said, "Do you want to come down and hang?" I was there. The only thing I can really remember about the sessions, however, was Marianne Faithfull—whoa. I thought, "This is the rock and roll mama of all time." And I was unabashedly just stricken. She was with Jagger. When she wandered into the room, I thought, "Oh, this is what the fuss is all about." She was some stone fox, I'll tell you.

-Mike Nesmith

Micky and I are meeting the Beatles at a London club called the Speak Easy. And in come George and John singing to the tune of "Hare Krishna," "Micky Dolenz, Micky Dolenz, Dolenz, Dolenz, Micky, Micky." And Paul is with Jane Asher and the other guys didn't bring anybody, and we carried on and chatted and shouted and screamed and I had just done some STP which was an LSD-type psychedelic drug. I mentioned it to John and he said, "We heard that's no good. Mama Cass told us not to take it." But he said, "Okay." So I went back to the hotel and I got some. Popped one down his throat. I guess he was alright because he seemed to survive. I don't think I'm responsible for "Strawberry Fields," though.

George Harrison was recording the music for the *Wonderwall* movie and he asked me if I would play the five-string banjo. I don't remember why I didn't have one at the time, but Paul had one, and George borrowed Paul's. My girlfriend was there with a camera. He said, "Turn up the lights so she can shoot." He was very thoughtful and considerate. The English are different.

-Peter Tork

I heard "Pleasant Valley Sunday" as Carole King's demo, and I felt it needed an intro. Around that time there was a Beatle song on the radio called "I Want To Tell You." I'd been hearing that for days, and one night I came up with a riff that was derivative of the one by George Harrison. I remember hearing George on a television show documentary, saying, "You pinch a little bit here and there." So, thank you, George, for the "Pleasant Valley Sunday" riff derivative. I taught it to Mike Nesmith and that's how the song began.

-Chip Douglas

MICKY'S STORY

It was the night after the party the Beatles had thrown for us, so we were all, shall we say, feeling no pain. It was a very colorful night. Nobody slept, and that next morning I ended up walking through Kensington Gardens, a big park where Princess Margaret lives. The night before, Princess Margaret had sent a formal note to the hotel management and to us saying that she couldn't sleep and could we keep the kids quiet, because these kids were in front of the hotel all day and all night chanting, "We love the Monkees." I was in my pure Indian, afghan leather, beaded bell-bottoms and tie-dyed silks from India. Now, over this $400 ensemble, I was wearing a sweater encrusted with cement that I had picked up at an excavation site that somebody had used to wrap around an old pipe. It was like the earth, you know, the people, the workers, and I was one of them. I walked in this park to get away and just to kind of space out. And I'm going, "Oh, the colors...oh, I'm one with trees and I'm one with the sky…" Kids were starting off to school, and a couple recognized me

immediately and came running over. There were only two or three and I felt like, "Oh, my children, my children, come here." I'm talking about the trees and life and children—but they want to know about the Monkees. Quickly it gets past the fan stuff, and they have no more questions to ask. We're hanging out, and we're like friends, these twelve and fourteen-year-old girls. One of them becomes my lieutenant. When other kids come running over, she stops them and says, "Take it easy, he's cool. Don't rush. You'll get an autograph, no problem." And she's working for me.

By eight-thirty in the morning, there are two or three hundred kids. They're on their way to school and they're all in their little uniforms. They've now backed me up against this tree. My lieutenant can't do anything else. They want me to sing, they want pictures and they want autographs. I said, "I'll tell you what, if you let me get over to that little bandstand," which was a couple hundred yards away in the park, "I'll sing some songs." "Oh, yeah, okay, okay." "But

you have to let me get over there." And so all my little lieutenants go out, "Don't touch him, don't touch him, come on…" This sea of kids parts, and I half walk, half run, and make it to the bandstand. They're quite happy now to just surround me because they know I can't go anywhere. And I start singing Monkees songs to them, and they start singing school songs to me. And it becomes this very touching moment.

The police show up and say that these kids have to go to school. The kids are going, "No, we want to stay here." And I start crying and I say, "This is like a meeting of the continents, this great ethereal, spiritual moment. We're singing; this is more important than school." Bob Rafelson, Bert Schneider and Jack Nicholson, who was also on the road with us at the time researching our movie, come out. Jack comes over and says, "Micky, you gotta let these kids go to school." "I can't, Jack, I want to sing…." Jack starts crying, and now the policemen are crying, and Bob and Bert and the kids are all crying. I finally agreed to go back to the hotel. "Okay, kids, I have to go back and you have to go to school." "No!!" And so like idiots, these police, and everybody, decide the best thing to do is for me to make a run for it. It was a stampede to the hotel. Kids were running and falling and crashing and grabbing and we got trampled. I got up to the top of the balcony of this hotel. It was like a scene out of *Evita*.. I'm going, "My children, my children… Bye…bye…off to school."

-Micky Dolenz

I'd go down to the set in the morning to photograph them. Each week it would be an amazing spectacle. One week it was set up like a harem, with veils and silks hanging from the ceiling, pillows all over the floor, and beautiful girls all dressed up in veils. You just never knew what it was gonna be. It might be a circus, a magician's place, or a racing car episode. The week's big scene would usually be shot on Monday. They'd get into the close-ups later. That's when there would be a lot of down time, so we'd usually roam around the lot. Micky and I used to climb up a ladder three stories high into the beams of the ceiling where they hung the lights. There were cat walks up there and you could walk around and spy on everybody. When we filmed outdoors on the Columbia lot in Burbank, it was especially fun. Every time you turned a corner you'd be in a different time and place; there was a Western street, a European street. We spent a lot of time exploring and climbing in those false-front buildings.

-Henry Diltz

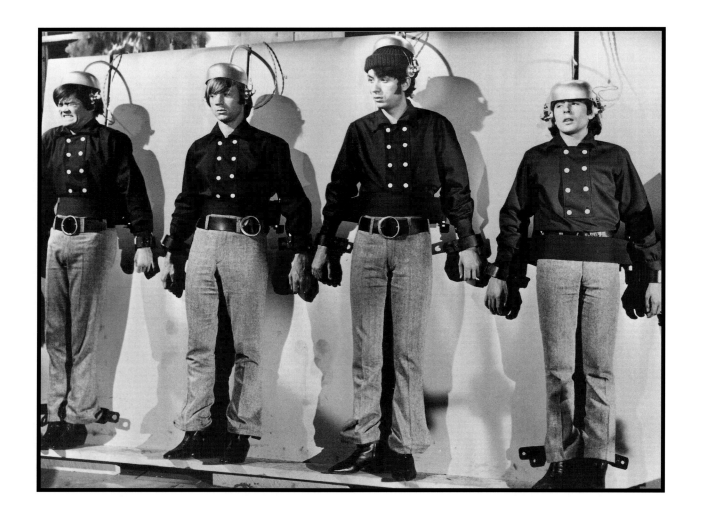

The heart of *The Monkees*s was *My Three Sons*. We lived like brothers, growing up and dealing with life. Although ours was uniquely set in the environment of the sixties pop scene, that had little to do with what the show was about. The plots of the shows were all about getting a job and Mike running for mayor and meeting some crooked toy manufacturer who was going to sell rotten toys to the kids and trying to solve social and moral problems. That's one of the reasons I think the show has stood up so well over the years, because it wasn't topical and the humor wasn't satirical.

-Micky Dolenz

I had mixed feelings about the Emmy Awards presentation. The show won Outstanding Comedy, and Jim Frawley won Best Director for a TV Series. He got up to accept his award and he said, "I just want to tell everybody, I just couldn't have done this without four very special guys and I'd like to thank them—Harpo, Chico, Groucho and Zeppo." He asked us beforehand if that was okay, and we all said "Yes." But I thought, "You know, there is buried in this remark the seed of something most profound." And I was interested to watch that grow over the years. So it wasn't a night of triumph for me; it was a night of a wake-up call that went off and I thought, "Oh, wait just a second here. This is TV, partner, this is media, which is the great American narcotic machine at work, and you probably need to pay some attention to what's happening to you and around you." So it was interesting. It wasn't even a pivotal moment, but it was a curious one.

-Mike Nesmith

We were filming interviews for the show. They said, "Let's roll." Davy got down on the floor and rolled. I looked at this kid and thought I've never seen anybody do anything nonsensical like that. I mean I was a goofy kid in a lot of ways, but only when I was confident. And here were these guys perfectly confident. The cameras were rolling. I was nervous as heck. And these guys were doing goofy things just like that. I learned a lot from them.

-Peter Tork

Davy, Micky and I were with a group of fans who won a contest to watch us film the show. Davy pulled out a breadstick and broke it over my head. Micky said, "I dare you to do that again." So Davy pulled out another breadstick and broke it over my head. Micky said, "Let me see you do that again."

Davy pulled out another breadstick and broke it over my head. Micky said to me, "Are you gonna put up with that?" So I took a breadstick and I broke it over Micky's head. We turned it around, that's the secret.

-Peter Tork

The reason that I was a teen idol was because I wasn't threatening. I'm a little guy and I'm not gonna jump on you and hurt you. It's funny, because there were a lot of guys who were my fans too, like a brotherly thing. The girls felt that way too. It wasn't a sexual thing with the Monkees, not the fans that were looking at me, anyway. When you become successful on a TV show like *The Monkees*, you become better looking, more intelligent, bigger in every way than you really are. The hardest thing was my family because they were bombarded by newsmen. When I visited my father, newsmen would rent a room in the house across the street, where they could wait there for me to come home and take pictures, knowing full well I was in the country and I'd be there. I had to climb over the back fence in a woman's dress and a scarf to get to my house. The fans knocked a wall down in front because they wanted the bricks. There's some girl in England who's got one of my bricks: "This is from Davy Jones' wall." It meant something to her and that's why she kept it.

-Davy Jones

I wasn't fond of what was going on with the teen magazines. I wasn't objecting to it, I was just uncomfortable with it. It seemed like the seedier side of show biz to me. I thought, "Why are they doing this? This is a good thing you got going here; the shows are good, the scripts are good, the people are good." The woman who ran *Sixteen* magazine would come around the set all the time with a camera, hanging over everybody. I kept thinking, "What a weird job." So one day a friend of mine came in and he said, "I was just in the supermarket and went to the magazine section. Do you know how many covers of teen magazines you were on?" I said, "No." He said, "Every single one."

-Mike Nesmith

I was a Beatles fan. When I had my newfound fame as a television star, I thought I'd figure out if I could broker this into a meeting with some people I wanted to meet. One of them was John Lennon. I flew to London and sent him a telegram that said, "I'm at the such and such hotel, and I would very much like to meet you." I signed it, "God is Love, Mike Nesmith." Now God is Love was an utterly radical thing to say in the sixties, especially on a telegram. He called me at the hotel. He said, "I'll send a car for you. Come stay with me instead." That was the beginning of the friendship. We maintained it from a distance. Every time I went to London I would look him up, and he would call me when he came here.

-Mike Nesmith

I asked Frank Zappa if he would guest on the show. He said, "I'll only come if I can have your part." And I said, "Well, that's fine. If you'll come on the show and be me, then I'll be you." So I dressed him up in a shirt and gave him a wool hat so he'd look like me.

My relationship with Zappa was never fully formed, so I have a distant love and great respect for the man. He was very kind. When people hated us more than anything, he said kind things about us. He was talking about the music, about how well it was produced and, "Did you hear that on the new Monkees album?" He offered to teach me to play lead guitar one time. It was an incredibly groovy thing to do. He worked with me for hours, but I never learned.

-Mike Nesmith

F ame is time-consuming. You often can't go where you want to. There was an extraordinary exhibit at the Chicago Museum of Modern Art in 1968. It featured a who's who of the art world of the sixties, including Kienholz, Oldenburg, Rauschenberg and Warhol. We all really wanted to see it but, of course, we couldn't. If one of us went some place, it was a traffic jam; if four of us went some place, it was gridlock. The museum staff was very gracious, and they let us in after hours. It was a very nice thing for them to do. I thank them after all these years.

-Mike Nesmith

JIMI HENDRIX

I saw Jimi Hendrix playing with a band at The Bitter End in New York. He was playing with, I think, the John Hammond Blues Band. He was just the lead guitar player. Somebody had said, "You gotta come down to the village and see this guy play the guitar with his teeth." That was his shtick. It was great. I didn't see or hear from him again until the Monterey Pop Festival. I was sitting in the audience with Ravi Shankar. I had on a full Indian headdress from the wardrobe department at Columbia. And I'm sitting there and Hendrix walks on the stage and starts playing the guitar with his teeth and I said, "Hey, that's the guy that plays guitar with his teeth." Of course he looked a lot different. In New York he had on jeans and a t-shirt and now he had on tie-dyes and paisleys and color and he's lighting his guitar on fire. I told the producers about him and he became our opening act.

-Micky Dolenz

I was in London visiting John Lennon, and I was having dinner with him, McCartney and Clapton. And John was late. When he came in he said, "I'm sorry I'm late but I've got something I want to play you guys." He had a handheld tape recorder and he played "Hey Joe." Everybody's mouth just dropped open. He said, "Isn't this wonderful?" So I made a mental note of Jimi Hendrix, because Lennon had introduced me to his playing.

The Jimi Hendrix Experience joined our tour in Jacksonville, Florida. They were the apotheosis of sixties psychedelic ribbon shirts and tie-dye, they had pinwheels for eyes and their hair was out to here. Jimi came wandering down our wing of the Holiday Inn, flanked by these big Southern cops. Jimi was diminutive; he was probably 5'6". These cops were towering over this trio as they walked down the hall, and I thought, "Man, I gotta see this thing live." So that night, I stood in front of the stage and listened to Hendrix at sound check. It was the first time I ever saw a Marshall amplifier stack, and they fired it up. He played the first couple of bars of "Hey Joe," and I was moved back physically about three feet; I had no idea how I'd gotten there. It was like gravity went away for a minute. And I thought, "Well, this guy's from Mars; he's from some other planet, but whatever it is, thank heaven for this visitation." And I listened to him play the sound checks and the concert. I thought, "This is some of the best music I've heard in my life." That night, he opened in front of us, and he walked into the beast. There were twenty thousand pink waving arms. He would sing, "Foxy" and they would shout, "Davy"—"Foxy"—"Davy…" Oh, man, it was a seriously twisted moment. He lasted seven dates.

-Mike Nesmith

icky and I went to the Monterey Pop Festival and saw Jimi play. Micky got it. I didn't. I did get it eventually. Micky said, "We gotta get this guy to open for us." Micky saw the genius and went for it. Nobody thought, "This is screaming, scaring-the-balls-off-your-daddy music compared with the Monkees," you know? It didn't cross anybody's mind that it wasn't gonna fly. And there's poor Jimi, and the kids go, "We want the Monkees, we want the Monkees." There were two wonderful things. One was that we went early to the show and listened to what this man could do because he really was a world class musician. If he'd been playing Beethoven, people would have been falling on their faces. And the other thing was, he was such a sweet guy that it was just a pleasure to have him around for company. His air of "everything's alright, things are cool" made you relax just to be around him. He taught me to play the vibrato on guitar. Jimi was just an angel.

-Peter Tork

We got to Chicago on the tour and found that Stephen Stills was staying at the same hotel as we were. The Buffalo Springfield were the group I had shot pictures of before the Monkees, so they were all good friends of mine. Micky, Stephen and I stayed up all night, talking and roaming around the hotel. The Springfield were playing a fair at an Indian reservation in Hayward, Wisconsin. Peter decided that we could use the Monkees' plane to fly up there. We all went— except for Mike—and Steve came with us. We were really into love beads at that point, and they had a lot of beads. We hung out all day and watched them do log rolling and different events and talked to the people and then came back.

-Henry Diltz

Jimi's on the road with us in Chicago, when we cross paths with Buffalo Springfield. Stephen Stills and Jimi Hendrix are sitting on a couple of hotel beds, jamming together. Micky was dallying with a woman over in the corner. He left her and picked up an empty guitar, put it in his lap, and started to wack a rhythm.

And then he stopped. Jimi reacted as if he'd been running and somebody belted him on the knees with a lead pipe. "What did you stop for?!" and Micky said, "I didn't know anybody was listening."

-Peter Tork

CINCINNATI

The coliseum in Cincinnati is off to one side of a plaza; the hotel's off to the other side. The subway empties into the plaza. We're getting ready for the show; we're all dressed up in our four matching suits and I've got on my green hat. We are "The Monkees!" We get in the elevator and just to be contrary, I push the close door button before anybody else gets on. We are now isolated from our security guard—just the four of us in the elevator, which is kind of, "Oh, isn't this fun—we're naughty little boys...." All we were about to do was descend into the jaws of our own fame. The elevator goes down and we realize we don't know where we're going. "Do you know where we're going? I don't know where we're going." The elevator goes down three floors and it opens to a kind of mezzanine foyer. It's empty. I stick my head out and the other three guys stick their heads out and we walk out of the elevator. I stand there and I say,

"Well, this is not the limo." We were supposed to go down, go through the wall of security men and get into the car. I start to get back on the elevator and the doors close. I walk out and there's the lobby, with about fourteen girls. And they look and see us and the chase is on. Whaaaaaaaa!!! Our natural instinct is to run. We go down the stairs and blast out of an exit door into the plaza, which is where all the people were coming for the concert. These girls were like a snowball, picking up more and more people. Thirty of them come out the door, and we're tearing across the plaza further and further into the mouth of the beast. And these girls are screaming: "Whooooo, Micky, Micky, Davy, Davy!" And you have to understand, if you get caught, it's not like you're a human being anymore; you're a souvenir. They don't care what part of you they take home. And it's not just clothing; we're talking about eyes and wisdom teeth and whatever

they can rip off. So we're dashing across this plaza and these people are screaming and everybody hears it now, and a thousand people begin to converge. All I see is a police car up ahead, and to me, it's a safe haven. I yell, "Police car!" We run over, slide into the back seat, and boom, shut the door. These two cops are sitting there having coffee and donuts. They turn around and look through the cage back at us as this sea of humanity sweeps over. The police car is rocking from side to side, faces press against the window. I said, "We're the Monkees, drive out of here!" They took us to the Cincinnati Police Station. They called the arena, and then took us in the back way. Sometimes it got right out of control.

-Mike Nesmith

We're on tour, in our hotel room, and there's a knock on our door. "Pizza's arrived." We said, "We didn't order pizza, but we'll have it—please come in." So they came in and they gave us the pizza. It's these two seventeen-year-old girls in pizza outfits—with little hats—the whole thing. Then they finally told us: they'd actually ordered the pizza to their room, bribed the delivery guys for their outfits and that's how they got in. And we thought that was a very original idea.

When we toured, we used to take whole floors. We used to wall creep—used to creep along the walls and get to gaps in the doors, pretending we were shooting each other and doing all kinds of things you only do when you're on the road. Our fans were so young, there weren't mass orgies going on or anything. It was kind of weird; my love life was like the Petrified Forest.

-Davy Jones

While on tour, we met the Beatles in London; they threw us a party and we got into the whole English mod-pop scene. When we came back to Los Angeles, if we were intolerable before, we must have been unbearable to work with because now we were pop icons. After partying all night in London with the Beatles, at eight o'clock in the morning we had to be back on the set. See, the Beatles and all the other rock groups got to keep partying, but we had to have real jobs. We had to show up and pretend that we were a rock group and be funny and bright and cheerful and polite and eight o'clock in the morning, all of a sudden, just got really early.

-Micky Dolenz

PISCES, AQUARIUS, CAPRICORN & JONES LTD.

Headquarters was the real labor of love for the Monkees. They wanted to prove to the world that they could play their own instruments, to prove that they could be a band. Once that was done, they began to do other things and began to get separated in their pursuits. Micky was always having parties, and Mike was always on the phone making business deals. It was difficult to get them all together in the same room to even talk about recording. So, for the *Pisces* album, I pulled in studio musicians to help get the tracks recorded. We'd have Peter and a drummer

named Eddie Ho and I still was playing bass and Mike would be there sometimes, but the basic difference I guess was that Micky wasn't so concerned about being the drummer. At one point we got Douglas Dillard to play the five-string banjo because he was the best player in town. The TV show was going on night and day, and they'd be busy or tired and one or two would show up and you had to do what you could do with what was available. I kept trying to get all four together but it was to no avail.

-Chip Douglas

After recording *Headquarters*, Davy didn't want to be banging the tambourine for fifteen to fifty takes every time we were working out an arrangement. It wasn't as if Mike and Micky and I got together and worked out the arrangements and then brought them into the studio, and Davy banged the tambourine for the two or three takes it took to record—it wasn't like that. We worked out the arrangements as we were setting them up. So with Davy, and with Micky's "I don't want to go back" routine, we had to modify our approach for *Pisces*. Even though at the time I had this dream to be in a real group, it was probably more about feeling a part of something. I felt that, as an actor, I was a hired hand. Having a voice in the recording process was for me to say I belong to this. For Michael it was about power. Michael came from an extremely poor situation. He told us that his mother would boil up a batch of liquid paper on the stove and he would go to Dallas and sell it, and they would eat that night on what he made that day. So it was pretty close. And so for Michael, it was about making sure everything was under control. Micky and Davy aligned themselves with us because they saw how important it was to us.

-Peter Tork

Paul Beaver played a relatively melodic Moog synthesizer, kind of a cake walk rhythm. The sound quality was a little unusual, but the pitches were just musical pitches. He played it as an instrument. Micky was one wild and crazy guy and he was willing and able to take the Moog into space. I think that's an example of Micky's genius. I didn't think a Moog was supposed to imitate a poor trumpet sound, which is how synthesizers are primarily used today. When I was at a party at Micky's, I brought a friend of mine along and said, "This is the Moog synthesizer, six big boxes and a keyboard. Micky plays it really well." Micky said, "Yeah, but you should hear it when it plays itself." He turned it on, and it played random oops and squeals and squawls, never repeating itself, until he turned it off.

-Peter Tork

"Daily Nightly" was a rambling comment on the Hollywood street scenes of the time, when people were meeting at Ben Frank's, and Pandora's Box had just burned down. That was a very important corner, where the people would congregate. They had set a bus on fire, which in turn burned down Pandora's Box. That was the first time that those crazy kids had gotten out of control! I was amused by the obvious inability of the press to digest this information. They just didn't have any sense of what was going on at all. So I just wrote it down in that poem.

-Mike Nesmith

Micky didn't want to play drums on the *Pisces, Aquarius* album. He said—these were his exact words—"You can't go back, Peter." Micky's major character flaw in my book is that he is afraid to revisit where he has done well. He wrote "Randy Scouse Git" and he never again went into heavy psychedelia. He was willing to take the beginner's luck that came to him. He's a brilliant guy, and he's willing to let his brain loose and flash out and act in unknown territory. But once he's done something good, he knows that his next three, five, eight efforts won't be as good because they won't have that newcomer's charge. So if he never goes near them again, he avoids the disappointment of not being able to do as well again, or at least for a little while and then accumulate the skills it takes to do better, and then go ahead and be brilliant beyond that. If Micky were willing to do that, I think he would be one of the world class artists of the day.

-Peter Tork

The tricky thing about the Monkees has always been that it wasn't really a group to start with, and most groups start with a singular musical vision. One man or woman, maybe two, have this vision of where they want to go musically and then they gather around people who become part of that vision, but there's usually just one captain of the ship. With the Monkees, there's always been four lead singers, four groups, four captains with very distinct musical tastes. I was Chuck Berry rock and roll, Mike was electro-country, Peter was down-home folk music, and Davy was flat-out Broadway. As long as we were given assignments to sing those kinds of songs, that was fine. When we did *Headquarters*, when we finally came together as this group, it was wonderful because that was the first time and about only time that these four kind of lead singers and four styles kind of merged and became one. After *Headquarters*, we figured, "Well, we've done that now." I know Peter wanted to continue in that vein, but the rest of us wanted to go off and become our own groups, essentially, and produce and write our own kind of music. The subsequent Monkees recordings became Micky and his vision, Mike and his vision, Peter and his vision, and Davy and his vision. The original Monkees music was Tommy Boyce and Bobby Hart much more than it was any of us. I sang the leads and Davy sang some of the leads, but that was the sound of Tommy Boyce and Bobby Hart and the songs that Don Kirshner chose.

-Micky Dolenz

During the second season, they got a soundproofed meat locker for us. We could turn up the amps and play loud music when they were shooting, and it didn't disturb the set. They didn't want us smoking dope on the stage, so we smoked back there where it was air conditioned. I ate lunch there, but I never did get it on with anybody.

-Peter Tork

The second assistant director thought, "We'll have four light bulbs inside and each one will have a name on it underneath, and inside the set on the stage there'll be four switches so all I have to do when I call one or more of them in, is flip these switches." Which was a great idea in theory. Of course, after you spend forty-five minutes in this vault with only the light of one candle, suddenly the 150-watt bulb goes on and you'd go, "Oh, no, no…" But it got us out of there and on the set. That's why in the second series you see us showing up in scenes like we don't know what we're doing. "Who are you? Oh, the camera…oh, okay, hi."

-Micky Dolenz

said, "How high are we lit over there?" The camera man would say, "How high do you want to be lit?" and he would say, "To the top of the balcony." The camera man and Micky would conspire to light the set where the spiral staircase goes up to the bedrooms. When filming commenced, unbeknownst to the directors, Micky would bypass the stairs, climb the wall and go up the balcony. That was Micky at his best.

People ask, "Why did Micky start curling his hair?" The truth is, he had been straightening it up until then. He looked more natural, and he was so much more natural inside his head. He really did find himself at that point. There were times when Micky

Micky was the lynch pin of The Monkees. As a visual comedic group, it was Micky who could go nuts, and who could trip out and deliver the lines. He was a genius when he was in his element.

-Peter Tork

We had all these little games that we used to play, and one of them was called Killer. You had three lives. You'd call "Hey, Micky!" and Micky would look and you'd go, "Bang!" Then he would have to fall and do a spectacular death, over chairs, whatever it might be. We'd just arrived in Australia and we were walking down the steps of the plane. I made sure I got down to the bottom real quick, first. Micky's at the top and I said, "Micky" and he went, "Oh, no…" I said, "Bang!" He does this spectacular fall all the way down the steps and the fans are going, "Oh, poor Micky." You had three lives and that's all you had for the whole game, and once you lost your three lives, you were out of the game, forever. To get in the game was tough enough, so nobody wanted to be out. It was the four of us, Bert, Bob, Ward, Jack Nicholson, and James Frawley. I remember when the game was over and it was because of Frawley. The second season was coming to an end. We were fooling around on the set, and Frawley shot himself three times and that was the end of his game. The Killer game ended, like everything else ended. We could feel it. "Hey, hey, we were The Monkees." It was coming to an end.

-Davy Jones

During the second season, I think people's attention was wandering. Bob Rafelson really wanted to make feature films. Bert was becoming increasingly radicalized, very interested in revolutionary politics. Each of the guys had developed more of their own aspirations, which were increasingly divergent from the Monkees. While we now see the second season of the show as having more character, I think the network perceived it as getting weirder and wondered what a third year would look like.

-Ward Sylvester

We were a pain in the ass. We did things that I look back on now with horror. I think Bert and Bob had love/hate feelings for us. They liked us because we weren't normal characters, and this is a case of taking the bitter with the sweet. You can have Hollywood-trained actors who know how to be quiet and sit still when they're supposed to sit still, and act when they're supposed to act, but you're not going to get crazies like us. I think they eventually got sick of it and didn't want to do it anymore."

-Peter Tork

I was used to being with professional actors, so there's a way of conducting yourself. I used to hang out with Judy Garland, Elizabeth Taylor, Dudley Moore and Georgia Brown and all these people on Broadway. We used to go straight off to Jim Downeys or Sardi's Steakhouse. I was used to being around adults. And all of a sudden I was put with these three other boys.

To me, it was always a job. I was playing the part of a rock and roll singer in a TV series. It gelled, and it worked for a long time until Micky wanted to direct and Mike wanted to write all the music and Peter wanted to play on all the records. I probably was a pain in the ass, too. When everybody started to want to do everybody else's job, that's when it became the deck hands taking over the ship. Our immaturity flared. We didn't behave like big shots; we never went around saying, "Do you know who I am?" and driving Rolls Royces.

-Davy Jones

JAPAN - AUSTRALIA

We were on the road in Osaka, and after all the furor that the Monkees aren't a real band, we caught fire. I remember the song we were playing, Mike's "Sunny Girlfriend." There was something about that song, and something about that feeling that just hit the pocket. It was wonderful. It was transportation. It was just the kind of thing that I got into music to do in the first place. And we're playing to 18,000 screaming kids and Davy's banging on the tambourine and he comes waltzing over to me right in the middle of this wonderful thing and he yells, "We're gonna form a group!" Which is why I love Davy Jones, because he noticed and he knew what it was about.

-Peter Tork

In Japan we had a threat on our lives by the communists. There was this communist cell that was concerned about, I guess, the corruption of Japanese morals by America. It also had something to do with building an airport outside of Tokyo. They cleared the streets and swept us into town with armed guards. Because we couldn't leave the hotel, vendors selling pearls, watches and clothes came to us. When we went to the concert, there was a lot of security. The concert was very strange. First of all, I was afraid I was gonna get shot. I had three more cymbals angled in front of my drums, as if little brass cymbals were going to stop a slug from a high-powered rifle. I was sitting back there behind these cymbals, barely visible, peeking out.

-Micky Dolenz

At the time, the guys were concerned whether the show was going to be picked up for another season, so they wanted to present the best tour that they could to up the interest. I don't think they had any idea how popular they were in Australia and Japan. When we arrived in Sydney for a press conference, it was unbelievable. We were swamped. It was media attention that they never had before. In

Melbourne, the fifteen miles from the airport to the hotel were lined with people welcoming their arrival. It reminded me of a presidential motorcade. We were just stunned.

We had a lot of equipment problems on that tour. In one of the shows—at Sydney—we started out with twenty-five amplifiers on stage that were supplied to us in Australia. We also happened to have brought with us from the States one bass amplifier, a prototype made by the Acoustic company. This was touted as the hottest new amplifier in the world, but this was the only one that existed.

The first thing that happened was at the Sydney airport. When they were unloading the equipment from the plane's cargo bay doors, they accidentally dropped the Acoustic amp—it fell thirty feet and landed on its head. We plugged it in later, and much to our surprise, it worked perfectly. At the concert, the Australian amps started blowing out within the first few numbers. By the time we reached the fifth song, we rigged the cords so that every piece of equipment was plugged into that Acoustic bass amp. And that's what we finished the show with.

-Bill Chadwick

H E A D

We'd been introduced to Jack Nicholson who, at the time, was an up and coming B-movie actor. Bob Rafelson had met him and they obviously got along real well, and he was introduced to us and we all just fell in love with him. We thought he was magnificent. He was a very charismatic man. Bob said, "This is the guy I want to write a movie we're gonna do." At the time, it wasn't called *Head*, it was called *Changes*. We had decided we didn't want to make a ninety-minute Monkees episode. In retrospect, that might have been more successful. So we all piled in Mike's limo, and met Bob, Bert and Jack at a golf resort in Ojai. For three days we got stoned and rambled into tape recorders. Out of that came the movie *Head*. Jack got writing credit and rightly so, because he did actually script it, but it was a real collaborative effort. I'm very proud of *Head* and the work I did in it. It's a marvelous, sixties, bizarre, episodic, strange film.

-Micky Dolenz

Nicholson was a gas. It took Nicholson's direction for me to get the gist of that speech that I gave after the guru's speech. Jack told me that he had written the speech largely from the only guy that he thought made any sense out of all those guru types, and that was Krishna Verde, who disclaims any guru role. If you read Krishna Verde now, he'll say again and again, "Don't follow me. Don't do things because I do them. Check out what I'm saying. If it makes sense, follow the truth as you understand it. Don't listen to me. Don't listen to anybody." And that has been a very strong beacon for me ever since. I never did fall into the sway of any guru. I was deeply distrustful of them at all times. One big Yogi guru said to me, "We must appeal to the one who knows," and he pointed up. And I'm going, "Is that where it all is, up there?" I mean, some people think that God is a honky on a throne directly overhead. Well you can't see him because the ceiling is there, but he's there, with a beard. The honky with the beard.

-Peter Tork

I loved playing "Circle Sky," live, in the *Head* movie. That was a high energy, garage band, power rock trio, with Davy up front playing the B3 organ and shaking the maracas—it was just cool. That was where it worked. Around that time, when we played live in Osaka, we particularly played good. If you could hear us, that's the way we sounded.

I think, had I had more to do with it, I would have pushed more into the surrealistic humor side. I only wrote one piece, and that was the Arab that rides up on the horse and says, "Pssst," and Micky walks over to him and the guy says, "Pssst," and rides off again. Now, I just thought that was funny. And that was the only joke I could come up with, so that's the joke I wrote and it did get into the movie. Had I had my way, I would have had a stack more of those in there.

-Mike Nesmith

The idea of the *Head* movie was that we had to break out of the black box which represented life. We all had different ways of getting out. Mike's way was to talk his way out, because he's the business man. Peter, Hare Krishna, water beds, brown rice, was to sort of levitate yourself out of the box. Micky was a jokester, and I had to fight my way out because I was always feisty. Being shorter than most, I always had to push my way forward. I had to let people know I was there.

-Davy Jones

BOB RAFELSON ON *HEAD*

Jack loves the *Head* movie. It's different from the Beatles' movies. It's intense and severe, and it exposes much of what all rock groups went through but nobody had the guts to tell. In the movie we saw the Monkees as victims. The energy had run its course with their old audience. We tried to reconfigure them for the more mature audience who had previously rejected them.

Head was the exposure of the whole myth: "Let's come out and tell the truth about having manufactured these guys and manipulated them."

All the way through, people are trying to sell them things. The weird guy in the black cape comes jumping down and says, "Think of the merchandising." Frank Zappa had a funny part in it where he came out and was talking with Davy Jones about how the eight-year-olds are counting on you to show them the way. By this time, the name Monkees was anathema to the public.

The movie explored techniques on film that hadn't been used before. The first shot of Micky under water is a perfect example. Now you see it on MTV all the time, but it was invented for the movie. We didn't have much money. The budget was $790,000, and it was shot in twenty-eight days. I got two long-haired kids out of UCLA who created effects that the established laboratory guys said couldn't be done. We invented double-matted experiences. Polarization hadn't been used in movies before. It took me six months to edit the film. When it was shown in France, the head of the Cinematheque overly praised the movie as a cinematic masterpiece, and from that point on, this movie began to acquire an underground reputation.

Even though we knew that this movie was an announcement of the end of the Monkees, we wanted people to see it. But we didn't know how to sell the movie because the Monkees had ceased to be on television and their record sales were declining. We wanted to see Marshall McLuhan, who at the time was a Professor of Communications at Fordham University. We met with his assistant and asked him, "How would you go about selling the movie since the Monkees' popularity is on the wane?" He said, "The best thing is don't tell anybody the Monkees are in the movie." We thought that was a good idea. They came up with this campaign to put a head on television with no sound and no writing. Everybody would be wondering just who is that, and ultimately we'd have a campaign that

said "Head." I went into the studio to have a picture taken of my head. I said, "Are you sure it doesn't make any difference whose head this is? As long as it's not a recognizable person?" He said, "No." So, I said, "In that case, why don't you sit here and I'll take your picture." John Brockman's head wound up on a poster and was broadcast all over television.

Because it was my first film, I was anxious. We went to the Columbia board room to meet with all the executives. They said, "Where would you like to have the film shown?" Keeping with the anonymity of not knowing whether the Monkees were in it and that sort of thing, I said that I would like to have it open at the Hudson Theater in Union City, New Jersey, where I used to go as a little boy. All the executives at Columbia Pictures thought I was deranged. They satisfied this

obligation by opening it instead at El Cinema, a Latin theater on 65th Street and Columbus Avenue in New York, where no English-speaking language film had ever been shown before.

Now, you can imagine there was a fervor of paranoia on my part that maybe we had gone too far with anonymity and nobody would go to see this movie. So, Jack and I decided to publicize the movie ourselves by walking through New York saying, "Did you see this remarkable picture called *Head*? It's amazing!" Instead of doing this in Central Park where we had now spread the word to maybe five kindergarten children, we decided that we would walk down 5th Avenue. We had little stickers made

up with "Head" and the same guy's face on them. Jack snuck up on a policeman who was giving a ticket to a guy who was selling chestnuts, and tried to paste a sticker on his white helmet. In seconds, we were up against the wall with guns out and we were arrested. I thought, "This is the very break we need. Producers and writer and director of film thrown in jail on day of opening." "You say you're the director of a movie," the policeman said to me. I said, "Yes...named *Head*." Jack was ready to go in the slammer. The policeman asked, "Where is your movie opening?" And I said, "Uh, ummm, uh, El Cinema Verite." Well, they put me in the pen, too. We were released just in time to see people beating up, literally, on

the guy who had sold them the movie tickets, for having frauded them into seeing a movie that didn't tell them that the Monkees were in it.

-Bob Rafelson

The television special *33 1/3 Revolutions Per Monkee* was very strange. It was produced by Jack Good, who had created and produced *Shindig!* I think it had some good moments. There was a remarkable sequence of Little Richard, Fats Domino and Jerry Lee Lewis playing grand pianos stacked on top of each other, which you aren't gonna see anywhere else. And I did some good work on it. But just before we were going to tape it at NBC, the musicians at NBC went on strike and shut down the studio. And so we had to do it by remote, and no one had ever done remote videotape before. Somebody had to put these huge Ampex video machines on some kind of refrigerator dolly and roll them onto the back of a big truck and truck them over to MGM, and then somehow hook up all the cables and the control board. Taping the show was an absolute nightmare. By this time, of course, we were also getting really jaded by it all. Bob and Bert were no longer interested; they never even showed up. I remember feeling uncomfortable about the whole manufactured Monkee thing, because by this time we were a hot little band. But I think there were some good moments in it.

-Micky Dolenz

When we did the *Johnny Cash Show* I established a friendship with him. I love Johnny Cash, he's a charming man. He called me up once from Montego Bay. "This is Johnny Cash speaking." I said, "Who is it really?" "No, it's Johnny Cash." I said, "Where are you?" He said, "Montego Bay." I said, "No, I know it's not Johnny Cash." He said, "Well, my granddaughter loves you and I want you to come and see her." And I said, "Well, I'll be in Nashville." He said, "I know you're gonna be there, boy, I'm comin' to see you." So we played Nashville and he came to see me and I went to his house and I've been there many times since, but he took me to his bedroom and Johnny and June have their own quarters, their own bathrooms—one for his and one for hers. It makes for a happy marriage. He took me to his bathroom, and I looked down and he's got a see-through toilet seat, with barbed wire in it. He said, "That's how I wrote the song, boy—I fell into a burning ring of fire!"

-Davy Jones

150

MEXICO

We got a call from a guy down in Mexico. "We want the Monkees to come play." "Well, it's thousands and thousands of dollars. How legitimate are you?" "I'm really legitimate." "Well, what's the venue?" "It's a 600-seat nightclub." "No, you don't understand—we would play the bull ring." He said, "No, you don't understand. For a nightclub, I'm gonna give you more than you ever made in any stadium you ever played." And the agent says, "Well, fly up here with the money in a suitcase," and the guy does.

We get down there and, for starters, the tickets were $1,000 a piece—that's not the real number, but it was some number like that. For another, he's selling bottles of champagne for like $1,200. His family's there, three little girls, eight, nine, and twelve years old, in crisp, white, crinoline dresses, and their hair all done up with tiaras. I thought, "This really has gone into the zone. I don't know what's happening here." As I live and breathe, I swear to you this is the truth, the parking lot was carpeted with red carpet, and its a 200-car parking

lot, too. We leave this club in Mexico City and travel to Guadalajara to play the bull ring, to fewer people, it seems, than saw us in the club. We're backed up by an all-black, ex-Ike and Tina Turner, James Brown-type band that Davy and Micky found, Sam and the Goodtimers. By now we are frilled and laced and the costumes had gotten more and more bizarre and I think I had little buttons on the hat that I'm wearing and it's just really gone into Marie Antoinette time. Afterwards, we go back to Mexico City and we got a day to wait before we play at this club again. We're staying at a hotel that's on the plaza, which is across from the President's residence. We get this call that says, "There's gonna be a student demonstration, so be careful because the President has given the order to the military to fire on the students if they get out of line." And of course this is mind-boggling to me because I'm down there as one of the Monkees. So the next morning I get up and I'm curious to know why the students are revolting. I'm watching through my

students are revolting. I'm watching through my window as buses arrive and uniformed guards line the square, shoulder to shoulder. Command centers are set up, but the students never materialize. It's an extraordinary view, and I think, "I'm gonna get my camera and take some pictures of this." With the long lens, I can see that the soldiers are in differing stages of disarray, which includes uniforms with missing buttons, things hanging off, belts askew, the wrong type of shoes, and so forth. I take a couple of pictures,

put the camera away, and there's a knock on my door. I open the door and these two guys say, "Were you just taking a picture?" I said, "Yeah." They say, "Let us have the film." And I said, "I'm not gonna do any such thing." And they say, "Give us the film right now or you're gonna go to jail." And I said, "I'm an American citizen. You can't do this to me." They come into the room. They get my camera, open it, take the film and leave. You cannot say "I'm one of the Monkees," and have it mean anything other than peals of laughter. Nobody's gonna say, "Oh, well, here's the film back." So I'm just mute. When I get to the club that night, I tell the owner. Now the club owner is a guy that I have no idea where his funds are coming from, I have no concept of his strata of international wealth; I've never encountered it before in my life. And certainly now, standing there in front of Sam and the Goodtimers singing to the twelve-year-olds and Mexican teenagers and their parents, I couldn't be more divorced from this culture. I didn't have any sense of what was going on. I told him, "A couple of guys came in and busted in my room and took my film." And the club owner said, "What?" And I said,

I'd mention it in passing." "Did they hurt you?" I said, "No, they just came in and stole my film." We played the show. I go back to the hotel that night, and there sitting with the key, is my canister of film. A note says, "We're very sorry for any inconvenience we may have caused you—Agents 42 and 37." It really says Agents 42 and 37, and it's in English. I thought, "This guy has got some kind of pull. There's some dynamic laying over this whole political structure down here I know nothing of." But I tapped into it. The guy carpeted his parking lot, he charged a thousand dollars to get in, he's flown the money up to get the Monkees to come down and play for him. The next morning there's a knock and I open the door and it's the agents standing at the door. Now the roadie has come in to get my luggage and they say in broken English, "Did you get your film back?" and I said, "Yeah." And one says, "Well, we're very sorry and we really hope that there's no problem." And I said, "No problem at all." And, of course, I don't know whether they've given me my real film

back; I want to get out of the country. They said, "Here, we just want you to know, as a token of our apology, please take this." They hand me a grocery sack, make a couple of bows and walk away. Now I can't immediately see what's in the bag because it's a plastic bag inside a large, brown paper grocery sack. I get inside the room, and the sack is full of cleaned marijuana. Absolutely to the top. I turn to the roadie and I say, "David, I just got handed a million dollars worth of marijuana by these two feds." He took it from me and ran into the lobby of the Plaza Hotel, picked up one of the seat cushions, dumped the sack and put the cushion back. "Let's get out of here," he said.

-*Mike Nesmith*

1986
REUNION TOUR

David Fishoff was primarily a sports agent who promoted our 1986 reunion tour. He grew up cloistered in an Orthodox household and didn't even know about the Monkees, because he didn't watch television or listen to pop music. He didn't know what he had. He was ready to put us in 500-seat clubs, until it exploded on him and we were playing 6,000 and 10,000 sheds and arenas. Boy did he luck out.

-Peter Tork

The 1986 reunion was amazing. I'd been living in England for over ten years, directing and producing television shows and nobody ever mentioned the Monkees. Michael Dolenz. I was going by the name of Michael at the time. And somebody had the bright idea to go back on the road for the twenty-year reunion for ten weeks. It was gonna be a ten-week little tour, small venues, just to have a little fun. I thought, "This will be great. I'll take the family on the road." Well, three years later, I'm still on the road, living out of a bus; it's ruining my family and destroyed my marriage and Peter and David and I are at each other's throats. It was very exciting. It was nice to kind of have a confirmation that there was something valid there, that the show had stood up after all those years; you could still watch it and get something out of it, that it was funny and it was good; that the songs stood up and the music stood up and people identified with the tunes and enjoyed them. What I find so incredible is that the TV show only lasted two years. I've had dinner parties that lasted longer.

-Micky Dolenz

I enjoyed guesting with the guys at the Greek Theater in 1986. It made me really want to go out and play. There are, maybe, two dozen Monkees songs that I really like playing. I never really quite understood why the place went so bananas for the Monkees. I mean, you sit and watch the Eagles—this fabulous, technically perfect band—but nobody's going bonkers. The Monkees concert is like a Grateful Dead concert. People go nutso. I don't know why. But it's nice to be a part of it.

-Mike Nesmith

I was producing a movie called *Square Dance* in Texas. It was a starring part for Winona Ryder, who was fourteen or fifteen. She said, "Aren't the Monkees gonna play in Arlington?" which was just up the road from where we were filming. I said, "Yeah." And she said, "Do you think you could get me tickets?" And I said, "Well, yeah, I probably could." And she said, "I'd really like to go—would you take me?" And I said, "No, I won't take you. I can't possibly do that." She said, "Why not?" I said, "Nonie, I am one of the Monkees. I can't show up in the crowd with you going to a Monkees concert." She said, "Well, I really want you to take me. That would really be fun for me." I was madly in love with her—she was such a wonderful, young girl. There's a certain age at which young women blossom; they have a puppy quality about them, very fetching. She was right at that age. I just couldn't say no to her. I said, "Let me see what I can do." I wrangled a couple of tickets, and they were real ordinary tickets. I didn't want box seats or anything. From the costume department I got a fat pad, and I grayed my hair and my beard. I put on a pair of old man's glasses and a baseball hat, and I took her to the show. We sat there with 25,000 people, after a ball game. They came out, and I was in the middle of the crowd, watching a Monkees concert. It wasn't really a Monkees concert, because I wasn't up there with them, but I could watch those guys play and I could listen to Micky sing and I could hear those songs on the stage and I got some inkling of what the whole thing was about. I wondered to myself if I could have ever been a Monkees fan, because I really liked that experience; I liked the way Micky sang, I liked the way Davy sang and the way he looked. I liked the love that was exchanged between the audience and the performers, and the reciprocity of it, which was complete. There was a lot coming off the stage from those guys, and a lot going back to the people. It was edifying on one hand, but on the other hand it was uplifting. I had never realized that that was going on at Monkees concerts because what I was trying to do was play loud enough so I could be heard. I think Nonie liked it as well.

-Mike Nesmith

P O O L   I T !
1 9 8 7

J U S T U S
1 9 9 6

I don't practice the tambourine often these days. Sometimes when I'm dusting I take it off the shelf, but dropping it doesn't count, does it?

-Davy Jones

My notion is that Rafelson and Schneider had what I'm fond of calling a "Gepetto Complex." They actually did want to see their little puppets become real live boys. We had "Pinocchio Complexes." We wanted to be real live boys, too.

-Peter Tork

Micky's said it entirely too often, and I hope he'll quit, that we were no more a pop group than Leonard Nimoy was a Vulcan. It's simply not true. We were far more a rock group than Leonard Nimoy was a Vulcan. We did play, we did perform, we did make music, and we've made music recently.

-Peter Tork

I have a very high regard for the fellows. Always have.

-Mike Nesmith

PHOTO CREDITS:

Michael Ochs Archives: pp. 8, 9, 11, 13, 14-18, 20-26, 28, 29, 31-34, 36, 38-41, 44-49, 51, 52 bottom, 53, 54, 56, 57, 59, 60, 67-71, 80, 82-85, 87-89, 90 bottom, 92, 93, 96, 101-103, 106, 107 bottom, 108, 110, 112-116, 118, 122 bottom, 126-129, 131, 135-137, 139-141, 144, 146-149, 153, 160.

Henry Diltz: pp. 6, 30, 37, 42, 43, 52 top, 58, 63-66, 73-79, 86, 90 top, 95, 97, 98, 105, 107 top, 111, 117, 120, 121, 123, 125, 130, 133, 138, 142, 143, 145, 155, 158, 159.

Mark Bego Collection: pp. 27, 122 top, 150.

Rick Klein/Gary Strobl Collection: p. 100.

Gary Strobl Collection: p. 109.

Brendan Cahill Collection: p. 152, 153.

Rhino Records: p. 81.

Henry Diltz for Rhino Records: p. 157.

Andrew Sandoval Collection: p. 72.

Interviews conducted by: Harold Bronson, Delilah Films (Chuck Harter, Stephanie Bennett, Alan Boyd), Andrew Sandoval, Eric Lefcowitz.

Photographic art prints of many of the photos used in this book are available by calling The Photo Department, 1-800-432-0020.

The Monkees' entire catalogue of albums and TV shows has been lovingly reissued on Rhino Records and Rhino Home Video. If unavailable at your local store, call Rhino Direct at 1-800-432-0020.